Rogue Elephant

and

Man-Eaters Don't Laugh

Rogue Elephant

· · · AND · · ·

Man-Eaters Don't Laugh

Two Missionary Adventure Stories for Children

CHARLES LUDWIG

Rogue Elephant

© 1954 by Scripture Press Foundation, Chicago, IL

© 1999 by King's Bookshelf, Belleville, PA

© 2018 by King's Bookshelf, Belleville, PA

Man-Eaters Don't Laugh

© 1967 by The Moody Bible Institute of Chicago

© 1999 by King's Bookshelf, Belleville, PA

© 2018 by King's Bookshelf, Belleville, PA

ISBN 0-9673806-1-8

Reprinted by permission

King's Bookshelf Publications

35 White Hall St.

Belleville, PA 17004

Contents

Rogue Elephant

PART I

A Missionary Adventure Story

BY CHARLES LUDWIG

1 Rogue Elephant

NDAMA squeezed Ochella's arm a little tighter as the loud crashing around them increased. He knew there were few animals in Africa big enough to break through the jungle as this animal was doing.

"We'd better head for the river," he whispered, peering cautiously into the jungle of sage and umbrella-shaped acacia trees. "If I'm not mistaken that's the Rogue Elephant!"

The brothers fled to a place of refuge behind some tall trees that line the Swam River, a crystal-clear stream that flows from springs on Mt. Elgon. The crashing in the bush increased and then a huge elephant stepped into the clearing where Bwana Paul's corn grew in long, green rows.

The elephant tramped through the grain, its large sail-like ears moving back and forth. It picked up several stocks of corn and threw them away. Then it noticed some native huts nearby. Without a moment's hesitation it put its trunk around the cone-shaped roofs and tossed them into the bush in much the same way as Ndama and his younger brother, Ochella, would skim a stone on a wide river.

A herd boy came along driving his cattle. Suddenly, seeing the elephant, he dropped his whip and with a yell of terror climbed a tree. But he had barely reached what seemed a safe position when the elephant saw him. It lumbered over to the tree, wrapped its trunk around the middle of it and started to shake it back and forth.

Ndama's eyes widened. He knew that elephants were strong, but he had never dreamed an elephant could shake a tree that was well over a foot thick. The elephant shook it one way and then another. The herd boy held on for all he was worth, screaming like a man in the jaws of a man-eating lion. The elephant paused, then it started again. This time it shook the tree so violently the boy was thrown from his perch. Fortunately he landed on soft ground, and was able to get up and flee to the river.

The elephant shook the tree some more, then it went after the cattle. It took hold of a cow by the tail with its trunk and pulled. The cow strained as hard as it could to get away. Then suddenly the elephant let go and the cow turned a neat somersault. Ndama had to hold his nose to keep from laughing.

The next cow wasn't so lucky, for the elephant charged it and drove one of its gleaming white tusks through its side. As the cow fell the elephant pulled out its tusk–now crimson with blood–and charged another, and then another–killing them all in the same way. By the time it was tired of this little game there were six dead oxen.

Not satisfied with this destruction, the elephant tramped through the corn, crushing it with its enormous feet, pulling it up with its trunk and throwing it in all directions. Then it turned its head toward Ndama.

As it advanced slowly toward him, its trunk extended and its ears nervously flapping, Ndama found himself staring at the largest animal he'd ever seen. It was so huge it looked like a walking fortress. He had heard of elephants with tusks that weighed over two hundred pounds. Such a size had seemed fantastic, but now as he watched this mammoth brute he knew it was true!

A Buganda had told him how he'd seen an elephant put its tusks under an Austin lorry (truck) and throw it into the bush with as little thought as one would discard a banana peeling. He had refused to believe this. But as he watched the approaching elephant he knew that such a thing was entirely possible.

Ndama wondered if it had seen him or if it just happened to be coming in his direction. If it attacked him he could see no possible way of escape. The trees were too thick to climb, and the water was too shallow to hide in. His only chance was to slip behind some foliage, and hope for the best.

The elephant came on, curiously shaking its head from side to side and making shrill noises–like the sound of a circular saw cutting into extra hard wood. Suddenly a little dog started to bark. The elephant stopped and listened. Then it pivoted on its feet and charged.

Up until now Ndama had not noticed that an old woman was sitting on a rock a short distance away. She was very old and her face was lined with deep leathery wrinkles. Her eyes were toward the charging animal, but they seemed to see nothing. She tried to hold her little dog, but it broke loose from the banana bark string and started snapping at the elephant's back legs.

As it approached her the elephant lowered its head and turned it slightly to one side. It struck the woman with its tusk, and then let out a shrill bellow of rage and retreated into the jungle.

When he was sure the elephant was gone Ndama ran over to the woman's side. He found that she had been terribly gored. Then he noticed the end of the elephant's tusk on the ground. It was about a foot long.

"I guess the rogue didn't see the rock," he said, picking up the broken piece of ivory. "We'd better call Bwana Greeni, and get him to take her to the hospital."

Their missionary friend was in the stone house at the

back end of the farm visiting with its owner, Bwana Paul.

"Bwana Greeni," shouted Ndama, all out of breath for he had run the whole distance, "a woman has been hurt by an elephant. We'd better take her to the hospital at Kitale!"

The elderly missionary ran his fingers through his thinning hair as the boys talked. "Where is she?" he asked, getting up and taking the lorry keys from his pocket.

"Down by the Swam River," said Ndama, leading the way to the old lorry.

The boys climbed into the crude cab and Ndama directed the missionary to the scene of the tragedy.

Green jumped out of the cab and felt her pulse. "I doubt if she'll live until we get her to the hospital," he said, biting his lip and shaking his head. "She's lost too much blood."

They piled some gunny bags in the back of the lorry and then lifted her in. As they laid her down Ndama saw the wound inflicted by the elephant, and he had to turn his head to keep from fainting.

"It was the dog that caused it," said Ochella, after they'd crossed the bridge that led to the dirt highway. "If someone doesn't kill that elephant he'll kill everyone around. I never knew an animal could be so mean!"

The road to Kitale was a rough one and full of holes, and twice Ndama and Ochella had to get out and push. Green drove as carefully as possible, but even so the lorry bumped terribly. They didn't get to the hospital until noon.

The boys who came out with a stretcher to carry her in were dressed in white shirts and khaki trousers. As they took her from the lorry Ndama heard one whisper to the other, "She's already dead."

The European doctor confirmed what Bwana Green had prophesied. "She probably died on the way over," he said, rubbing his trim black goatee. "But it was certainly good of you to bring her in. You may not know it but we've had six people here in the last week who've been wounded by elephants. I wish someone would do something about it!"

Instead of driving straight home the missionary went over to the game warden's office. A Goanese clerk met him at the desk.

"I'm sorry," he said, after Green had indicated his wish to see the warden, "but Bwana France is at home ill with malaria. You'd better come see him some other day."

"What is his address? I must see him!"

"He's very ill."

"What's his address?"

The Goanese wrote it down on a slip of paper and handed it to him. "Bwana France won't like this," he murmured, a big frown covering his oily face.

Without answering Mr. Green drove over to the warden's home. He pulled into the red murram driveway, and parked in front of the white stucco house. "You stay here," he said to the brothers, "while I talk to Bwana France."

He disappeared into the house and was gone for the better part of an hour. When he came out he asked the boys to go in with him.

Bwana France was propped up in bed on several huge pillows. There was a bottle of quinine and a glass of water next to the kerosene lamp on the table by his head.

"The warden tells me that this rogue elephant has been destroying gardens, killing cattle and human beings for a long time. He would like to go out and kill it himself but he can't because of malaria. He has now suggested that we go and get it. But since it's such a dangerous rogue we thought we'd give you a chance to refuse. This elephant is a vicious one and if we go after him we may not return. What do you say?"

The brothers were silent as they turned this over in their minds.

"I told Bwana France," continued the missionary, "that you are the bravest boys I've ever had. I mentioned how you killed the man-eating lion in the Suk and also how you killed the black-maned brute on the Masai plains.* He will give us a letter with permission to kill it and we won't have to buy a license. Of course, the ivory will all belong to the Crown, including the piece the rogue broke off on the rock."

Green might have said more, but Ndama interrupted him. "I'll go," he said eagerly.

"How about you?" asked Green.

"If Ndama wants to go I'll have to agree," said Ochella with a wry smile.

"Elephants are peculiar animals," said Bwana France, speaking in Swahili so that Ndama and Ochella could understand. "If they kill their first victim one way they usually use the same method on all the others. Once in the Congo I shot an elephant that had been causing a lot of trouble. This elephant killed people by stamping on them with his back legs. There was usually nothing left of them by the time he got through–that is, nothing but a flat mass of blood and bones. He was a regular fiend! The elephant you're going after on Mt. Elgon kills people with his tusks. Sometimes he charges his victims, driving a tusk through their stomachs as he did to this old woman. Other times he picks them up in his trunk and rubs them against his tusks. I know all of this because I saw the people that were brought into the hospital. And so if you want to eat any more flying ants you'd better stay out of his reach!"

The heaviest rifle Green had was a .303 British Army rifle, so he borrowed Mr. France's .375, together with twenty rounds of ammunition.

Green stopped in the Indian bazaar (business district) and loaded up with supplies for the coming safari. As the Indian trader packed the canned goods into a wooden box Ndama recalled how one of the Masai had insisted that the

---

*Read about this in *Man-Eaters Don't Knock* and *Man-Eaters and Masai Spears*.

cans were the eggs of some strange birds that lived in the land of the white man.

They also bought a small sack of posho (cornmeal) to make obusuma (mush) for Ndama and Ochella.

On their way home Green suggested, "If either one of you boys wants to stay on the farm just say so. I don't want to force anyone. This may be a long safari. The loads will be heavy and there will be much danger. It may take us many, many days before we catch up with this rogue. But I have a feeling that if we kill it we may be able to tell the people about the Lord Jesus Christ. Also I want you to remember that we'll have to go through portions of the Gishu tribe. The Gishu used to be cannibals. And I think that there are some of them alive even now who've eaten people. The only reason they don't kill humans for food now is because they are afraid of the government. But, of course, if we go way into the interior of their country they might try to eat us, thinking the government would never find out."

He paused long enough for all of this to sink in. Then he said, "If you want to stay home say so now."

"We will go with you," said Ndama. "We're not afraid of danger. God will take care of us!"

They went back to the place where the woman had been killed and examined the ground. "The only thing to do," said Green, "is to follow the spoor. This will be a hard job, but I think it will be the best way."

The boys divided the load between themselves, carrying the packs on top of their heads. Green led the way, following the easily seen elephant tracks. In the places where the soil was soft the tracks were so deep they had to be careful not to stumble into them. They led into the bush that skirted the west side of the farm.

"Maybe we should go back and cross the bridge and find the spoor on the other side of the river," suggested Ochella.

"If we do that we'll lose the tracks," replied Green, shifting the heavy .375 from one shoulder to the other. "Without a doubt we'd find tracks on the other side, but those might belong to another elephant. I'm not just interested in killing an elephant. I can do that any day of the week. I want to kill the rogue elephant, and I'm not going to stop until I have."

"But how will we cross the river?" asked Ochella. "Maybe it's full of crocodiles!"

"The Swam is too shallow for crocodiles," replied Green.

The spoor led to the river, and the party had to go downstream a few yards in order to cross on some conveniently placed stones.

On the other side of the stream the spoor led almost directly to the base of Mt. Elgon. Ndama and Ochella did their best to keep up with their missionary friend, even though the sweat was making tiny rivers down their spines. They stumbled on, over rocks and ravines, through wait-a-bit thorns, and up steep canyons until evening. By this time they were climbing the gentle slopes of the mountain. The natives they passed told them that soon they would be entering the bamboo forest.

Green kept going until it was dark. Then he stopped on a ledge of rock overlooking a small spring. "We will stay here until morning," he said. "Ndama can get our food ready, and Ochella, you can get some firewood. We'll have to sleep in the open, and since there may be lions around I prefer to have a fire burning while I'm asleep."

Gathering wood was an easy task. The country was full of it, and so it wasn't long until a big fire was burning.

Ndama got out some pots and pans and began to prepare coffee and beans and bread for the missionary. He built a separate fire and made obusuma for Ochella and himself. When everything was ready they washed their hands in the spring and bowed their heads while Bwana

Green asked God to bless their food and protect them on their journey.

The obusuma was especially good. Ndama didn't know whether this was because of his ravenous hunger, or because he was really developing into a good cook. He took handful after handful, worked it into his practiced palm until it was of a size that could be squeezed into his mouth, and then chewed it noisily. He was in the act of taking another handful when a native stepped out of the bush.

He was completely naked except for a brown blanket loosely wrapped around his body and tied at the left shoulder. There was a crude, petal-shaped spear in his hand, and an empty tomato can in the lobe of one ear. He stood there silently while they ate.

Ndama greeted him, and then asked him what he wanted.

2 Ungrateful Thieves

IWOULD like a job," replied the man in faltering Swahili."

"Ask him what he'd like to do," said Mr. Green.

Ndama put the question to him, and he replied, "I'd like to help carry the loads."

"Tell him to bring a friend and they can both have a job," said Green, pouring himself a third cup of coffee. "But tell him that if he works for me he'll have to stay with us until we kill the rogue elephant."

Ndama translated this and the man smiled. "We'll stay with you to the end," he said. "We're very happy that you've come to kill the elephant. It has been tramping down our gardens for a long, long time."

"Tell him to come here early in the morning, just as the sun is getting out of bed," said Green.

The new workmen were there in the morning, and Ndama learned their names were Kisu and Chumvi. They picked up the loads, placed them on their heads, and the party was on its way to follow the elephant's spoor.

As the day progressed they found themselves climbing higher into the mountain. Toward noon they came upon a colony of baboons. The humanlike animals scattered as if a fiend was after them and climbed on top of the nearby rocks and trees. One of them had a baby in her arms. She looked at the party through her black eyes and showed her teeth.

The spoor became harder to follow all of the time, and a little after noon they lost it altogether. Fortunately, however, there was a village just ahead, and one of the younger men came out and told them that he'd seen a big bull elephant with a broken tusk the day before.

"Where did it go?" asked Ndama, eagerly.

The man pointed to a place beyond his village. "It went there," he said.

Green followed his directions. At first they didn't find any sign of the beast, and then Ochella noticed where some heavy grass had been tramped down. He led the way to the spot and they found fresh elephant tracks.

"I wish the old rogue would choose a decent place to walk," said Ndama, gingerly pulling his khaki trousers away from some wait-a-bit thorns.

"What you should do," put in Ochella, "is to provide the elephants with a map, and direct them to walk on the highway!"

All at once Ndama yelled, "Stop!" And in less time than it takes to write it there was an arrow on his bow string.

Ochella laughed and took a step forward. "Stop!" commanded Ndama again. "There's a cobra, and he's about to strike you!"

The cobra slithered across the grass towards Ochella. It lifted its head, and opened its bonnet to strike. But Ndama was too quick for it. His arrow hissed through the air and cut its head off just below the neck.

Ochella jumped. Then his legs got wobbly. "Thanks, Ndama," he grinned.

Ndama picked the snake up by its tail and threw it down the mountain. "If you'd been bitten," he said, "you'd have been dead in ten minutes!"

Kisu and Chumvi looked at Ndama with admiration.

"Your arrow was quicker than the fangs of a snake," said Kisu, shaking his head and clicking his tongue.

They stopped for lunch, and then continued on until dark.

Green chose a camping site on the edge of a large forest of big trees. There wasn't any water at hand so Ndama had to go in search for some. He didn't like to look for water when it was dark, but this was the only thing he could do. He followed the fringe of the forest until he came to a path that led to a little valley. The path, Ndama reasoned, must have been an animal path because there were no villages nearby, and because it was covered with many animal tracks. Some of the footprints looked like those of a leopard!

Ndama knew that leopards like to go to the springs in the early morning, and in the evening just as the sun goes down. He wished he didn't have to get it, but he knew it was impossible to cook without water.

He tightened his hold on his bow as he followed the path. It was so dark he could hardly see, and he knew that if it weren't for the fire at the camp it would be impossible for him to find his way back. He continued on, feeling his way with his feet.

The little valley was steeper than he had thought, and he had to be careful not to lose his footing. As he descended toward the water he could hear gurgling below. There were tall trees on each side of the little stream and their moving shadows were ominous in the growing darkness.

He became sensitive to every sound. Once when he stepped on a brittle twig he jumped as if he had been charged by an incensed rhino. The little path turned sharply to the left just before it reached the water. Suddenly, while he was making this turn, there was a slight cough ahead of him. Without a moment's hesitation Ndama dropped the water bucket and climbed the nearest tree. Safe on a high branch, he looked down to see what it was, but darkness, complete darkness had come and he couldn't see a thing, not even the ground around him.

The coughing continued, then the shrill cry of a hyena that had caught the scent of death, cut through the air. This was followed by the doglike bark of a zebra stallion, then the distant, rumbling roar of a hungry lion.

Ndama sat in the tree in total darkness. He knew if he climbed down he would meet certain death, but, because of the blackness, it was impossible to know what would cause his death. A lion, he knew, would probably break his neck with a blow of its powerful forefoot. A buffalo would simply toss him into the air with one of its long, curved horns, and then trample him to death when he hit the ground. Leopards, he had heard, stand up to their victims, tear the flesh from their foreheads down over their eyes, and then maul them to death. And since they generally don't eat human flesh they just leave the mutilated bodies on the ground for the hyenas, or worse still, the vultures–Africa's efficient cleanup squad.

Soon a full moon climbed over the horizon and flooded the land with long, grasping fingers of eerie, yellow light. The dark river became a thin silver stream and bending its head, right beneath him, was a full-grown leopard!

The leopard lapped up the water in the same way that he'd seen a cat quench its thirst.

The leopard, he knew, could leave the water and be up in the tree in less time than it takes for a Bunyore woman to spit after she's smelled something bad.

The spotted cat switched its tail and lapped up some more water. Then it silently disappeared into the dark shadows. Its place was now taken by a large, brown waterbuck. Ndama was surprised that such a cow-like animal with only horns to defend itself would come to the river just after a leopard; but there it was, as plain as day. Some ants started to bite him, squeezing their sharp jaws through the most tender parts of his skin. Then a tsetse fly drilled into his neck. Its bite was like that of a red hot needle suddenly pressed through the skin. He hated these flies because of the pain they caused, and because Bwana Green had taught him they carried sleeping sickness, a disease that is very hard to cure. He turned his head as he slapped at the fly, and then his heart stood still.

For sitting on the next tree, less than five feet away, was the leopard that had just had a drink. It watched Ndama closely out of its sad, yellow eyes. And as he lowered his arm the spotted animal let out a deep, anger-filled growl. There were several drops of water on the white fur under its chin, and its whiskers were long and white and had a damp look about them.

As Ndama looked into the big eyes, glowing grotesquely in the moonlight, he wondered what it wanted. He knew that leopards seldom attacked humans unless they were cornered. He was afraid to move his eyes or even turn a finger, for fear the leopard would consider it a hostile move and attack.

Ndama's lips didn't move, but a thought prayer was racing through his mind, and this prayer gave him the calmness he needed.

The leopard snarled, showing long, white fangs, as if challenging him to make a move. Then it closed its mouth and continued to stare.

Ndama prayed again, "Oh, God, help me out of this so that I can get down and take some water to Bwana!"

The leopard yawned widely, and then, with a great look of contempt on its face, climbed down the tree and trotted off into the darkness.

Although it was a foolhardy thing to do, Ndama descended from the tree, picked up the bucket, filled it with water, and started back to camp. As he walked along the path the sounds of the jungle filled his ears. He knew he was a fool for taking such a chance. But he was afraid Green and Ochella would be hunting for him and he didn't want to cause them any inconvenience–especially on the first part of their trip!

A cool breeze blew through the grass and he was thinking about the leopard and his chances of getting home again when something struck him a glancing blow in the face. His knees buckled under him and he spilt half the water. A cold sweat came out on his forehead. He had no idea what it was. Then a black shadow moved by in front. He lifted his eyes, and saw a harmless owl circling around!

As he proceeded up the path the sounds of the jungle increased. A laughing hyena howled in such a mocking way he felt chills go up his spine. He had a great urge to run. But he knew this would be a foolish thing to do. No one who knew the perils of the jungle ever ran. The jungle is a place where one has to use his head instead of his feet.

He was in sight of the fire when his attention was turned by a heavy crashing in the bush. He whirled to see what it was and found himself looking at a two-horned rhino! The rhino must have seen him at the same time, for it lowered its head and began to paw the ground.

Ndama had never seen a rhino before, but he had been told that they are exceedingly cruel and exceedingly fast, and that the only way to get away from them is to depend on their poor memory. If a buffalo charged you could sidestep just before he got to you. But the buffalo would remember, quickly pivot and charge again. Not so with a rhino. If you could get out of the way of one of these brutes it would pass and forget completely why it had charged.

The rhino came after him, its pig-like eyes gleaming in the moonlight. Never had Ndama seen or even heard of such a ferocious charge. The big pachyderm came thundering through the bush with the speed of a lorry. Only instead of avoiding the rocks and trees that were in the way as would the sensible driver of a lorry, the murderous thing came straight on—kicking over rocks and trees and everything else that got in its way.

He knew that there was just the right time to sidestep

the determined thing. If he dodged too quickly it would swerve and get him, and if he was too late he would be caught on the sharp end of the murderous horn.

Then it happened.

Ndama waited until the very last moment and jumped, but a small bush kept him from going as far as he should. The long horn picked him up by his trousers and he found himself being carried along at a terrific speed.

His first fear was that his trousers would tear and he would fall under the thundering feet. But by some miracle he managed to get hold of the short horn and hold himself on the rhino's head. When he traveled through the bush he had to be careful of thorns and trees. But the beast that had him had never heard of such refinement. It continued on in its terrible rush, driving its head through anything that might be in the way.

Ndama knew that there was only one way of escape and that was to throw himself on top of the rhino, and then slide down its back and off its tail. But he also knew that this was easier thought than done. The rhino was slowing down a bit, and Ndama figured it was because it was getting tired. He put both hands on the little horn and threw himself forward.

This was probably the hardest thing he'd ever done in his whole life. He knew that he would never get onto its back unless his trousers tore, and now, for the first time since he'd started wearing khaki pants, he hoped that the seat in them was thin. Fortunately the cloth was old and tore. But instead of landing on its back as he'd hoped he merely landed on its neck. And to make matters worse the rhino seemed to know that he was there, for it started to shake its head back and forth, and then up and down. When it threw its head upwards its horn went into Ndama's stomach.

Thinking quickly he grabbed a fold of the heavily wrinkled skin on its back and pulled himself forward until he was sliding down its spinal column. When he got to the tail he jumped as hard as he could, hoping to miss the back legs.

He landed in some wait-a-bit thorns with a thud, and the rhino continued on, its horn lowered to kill anyone who was unfortunate enough to get in the way.

Getting back to the original animal path wasn't an easy thing, for the rhino had carried him farther than he had thought. And when he got back he couldn't find the bucket or the bow and arrows. But he knew the danger that lurked behind every rock and every bush, and so he headed back to camp, hoping that a man-eating lion didn't eat him on the way.

Ochella, a blazing firebrand in his hand, met him outside the camp. "Where have you been all this time, and where is the water?" he demanded.

Ndama pointed to his torn trousers and the scratches on his arms and legs. Then he sat down by the fire and calmly told him the story. Ochella found it hard to believe. But when Ndama insisted that it was so he said, "Well, I guess it's true. If you could escape from the jaws of a man-eating lion you could escape from a charging rhinoceros!"*

"Where is Bwana Greeni, and where are Chumvi and Kisu?" asked Ndama.

"Just after you left," replied Ochella, "Chumvi and Kisu ran off with the food!"

"You should have kept an eye on them, Ochella!"

"We were gathering firewood. When we returned they were gone!"

"Where's Bwana Greeni?"

"He's out looking for them."

"What are we going to eat?"

"I don't know," replied Ochella, shrugging his shoulders.

The roar of a lion drifted into the camp. Ndama put some more wood on the fire, and a stream of sparks blew upwards. Then he pointed to his torn trousers. "There was

---

*This story appears in *Man-Eaters and Masai Spears.*

some thread and a needle in the food box, now what am I to do?"

Ochella examined the tear. "The only thing I know is to fix it together with some thorns!"

"What an idea," exclaimed Ndama. "If you had to sit in them you'd never think of such a thing."

Another lion roar rumbled into the camp.

"That sounds like he's pretty close," said Ochella. "I wonder if it's a man-eater."

A loud noise behind made them jump. Ndama spun around to see what it was, then a calmness came into his face. It was Bwana Greeni.

"Did you find Chumvi and Kisu?" asked Ndama.

"I found Chumvi," replied the missionary, wearily sitting down.

"Why didn't you bring him back?" asked Ochella.

"I couldn't. A man-eating lion ate him! There's nothing left but a few bones. Even our food is gone!"

3   The Honey Bird

OES this mean that we'll have to return to Bunyore?" asked Ochella.

Green shook his head. "We're not returning to Bunyore until we've killed the Rogue Elephant!"

"But what will we eat?" asked Ndama, hungry in spite of all the excitement.

"The Lord will provide a way," said the missionary confidently. He took out the Gospel of John and read the 14th chapter. Then he knelt with the boys by the fire and pled for God's protection. When they got up he said, "Now let's go to sleep. Tomorrow we'll need all the strength we can get."

Trying to sleep on such a night was like trying to tame a man-eating lion. Ndama always welcomed adventure, but a trip on a rhino's horn, and sleeping within a few yards of the place where a lion had just eaten a man, was just too much adventure. He wondered what they would eat. Of course, the country was full of game, but he knew Bwana Green only had twenty shells and that these shells should be saved for the rogue elephant.

Sleep finally came, but it was just before dawn. It seemed he had only closed his eyes when he was awakened by the missionary. "We'd better get on our way," he whispered.

"The first thing we should do," said Ndama, "is to find my bow and arrows. They may come in handy!"

Ochella and Ndama both searched for the missing weapons. And if Ochella had any doubt about Ndama's rhino trip those doubts were removed when he visited the place. A heavy swath of grass had been tramped down along the route the pachyderm had taken. And some of the trees that had been pushed down were as big around as the calf of his leg.

They started their search at the animal path and continued on in the direction the rhino had gone. "I think I dropped them the moment the rhino caught me," said Ndama, pushing the grass back here and there.

Suddenly Ochella lifted up the bow and three arrows. "These are still in good shape," he announced.

A little later Ndama found five other arrows, including three poisoned ones, and the bucket. The bucket had been stepped on, and was a little out of shape, but there were no leaks in it.

He and his brother quenched their thirst at the stream, filled the bucket and joined Green who was searching for the elephant's spoor. Finding the spoor wasn't an easy task. The dryness of the country made it hard to see even the heaviest tracks. It wasn't until the sun was halfway up in the sky that Green announced the direction they would take.

"I'm hungry. Shouldn't we shoot something first?" asked Ochella.

"We'll see something on the way," said Green.

They followed the spoor until noon, by which time they were all so hungry that they found themselves looking for game more than concentrating on elephant spoor.

"The deer will never come out in this heat," wailed Ochella, wiping the sweat from his face with a crooked forefinger and snapping it on the ground.

"Don't give up so quickly," chided Ndama. "We don't have to eat until evening. The fatter you get, the more of a temptation you are to the man-eater!"

They crossed a dry riverbed, climbed a small hill and

then worked their way through a patch of jungle. There was no doubt now that they were on the right track. Small trees and bushes had been recently tramped down in the jungle. Indeed there was one wide place where everything had been so thoroughly crushed it looked like the beginning of a highway.

"A cow with a little one must have spent the night here," said Green, surveying the damage. "An old elephant hunter told me that when a lady elephant with a young one puts up for the night she turns around about twenty times in order to kill any snakes that might cause trouble."

"I'm sure no snakes could have lived through that!" commented Ndama, whistling softly.

The sun had reached its zenith and had started to go down long before they saw their first game, a little brown dik-dik. Green raised his gun to fire.

"Don't waste a shell," cautioned Ndama. "Let me get it with an arrow."

Ndama stalked the tiny deer-like animal by slipping from one tree to another. He knew that he could probably get it from his original position if he used a poisoned arrow. But if he did this it would be necessary to cut out a large portion of the meat, where the arrow went in, and throw it away. The best way was to creep up close enough to drive a regular arrow through its heart.

He stepped on a dry limb and the moment it snapped the dik-dik lifted its head, its dark eyes shining. Ndama aimed, pulling the sinew string back to his ear. Then he lowered his bow. The dik-dik was looking right at him, and he didn't have the heart to kill it! He clapped his hands and it escaped into the bush.

"Why did you do that?" asked Ochella. "Don't you know that my stomach is as empty as a leaky cooking pot?"

Ndama shook his head. "I just couldn't kill it. Its eyes were so big and kind and its little horns were so pretty!"

"We'll see something else," said Green, "and then if

Ndama's afraid to kill it, I'll use my gun!"

While they were talking, a little honey bird flew overhead.

"Look at that!" exclaimed Ndama. "We'll follow it, and it'll lead us to honey. I'd much rather eat honey than dik-dik meat!"

The little bird flew ahead of them and then settled on the lowest limb of an acacia tree.

Ndama and Ochella ran up to the tree, but there were no bees or honey anywhere near them.

"Honey Bird, you've told us a lie," said Ochella, squinting through the sun at the little feathered guide. "Take us to some honey and we'll leave you some."

The bird flew on in front of them, leading them to some large rocks in a narrow valley. Here it flew around in a circle and then settled on the edge of a crevice between two large boulders.

Ndama slipped up to the rock and peered into the crevice, and sure enough, there were bees flying around inside and he could see the thick honeycomb. "Thank you, Honey Bird," he said. "Thank you very much!"

He looked between the rocks again to see how he could get at the comb. He had hoped that he could go around to the end of the boulders and walk into the crevice and take the honey from a standing position. But this was an impossibility. The honey was well beyond reach from both the top and the bottom.

"The only way we can get the honey," he said, "is for you to let me down between the rocks with a piece of rope."

"But we don't have any rope," said Green.

"That's all right," returned Ndama, "I'll find a green vine. You can let me down with that. Ochella, you go and get some grass and we'll light a fire and smoke them out."

"How are you going to light it?" asked his brother. "The thieves ran off with the matches."

"You get the grass, and I'll get the vine," said Ndama,

scratching his head. "By the time you get it here I'll think of a plan!"

The vine was harder to get than Ndama had thought, but he found one after a long search and brought it back with him to the rocks.

"Now, how are you going to build the fire?" asked Ochella, as he placed a long bundle of dry grass on the ground.

"Get me a dry piece of wood and I'll show you."

While Ochella was looking for the dry wood Ndama loosened the string on his bow. He cut the head off one of his poorest arrows and twisted the remaining shaft into the bowstring. Next he selected a short piece of flat wood and gouged out a socket in the center, making it just the right size to fit the notched end of the arrow. Then he crumbled some dry leaves and put them on the wood Ochella brought.

He placed the end of the arrow on the wood, and pressed it down with the piece containing the socket. When he pushed the bow back and forth the arrow whirled and soon tiny bits of hot ash piled up around the point. As the pile got larger Ndama blew on it until it burst into flame.

"You're smarter than I thought you were," said Ochella, touching a bundle of grass to the tiny flame.

"Don't say that until I get the honey," returned Ndama. He wrapped the end of the vine around his shoulders and tied it, with the knot on his chest. "Let me down carefully," he said. "And when I jerk the vine three times pull me out. I can stand a few stings, but not too many."

He put an extra bundle of grass in his mouth and eased himself over the ledge. He found that the crevice was narrow enough for him to place a foot on each side. This made things much easier. He worked himself down until he was in reach of the honey. Then he put the burning grass to the bees.

The bees hummed angrily and a number of them got through the smoke and stung him, but he was so hungry that he didn't care. He moved the flame back and forth across the comb and smiled as the bees moved out of the way. By now he could see that the comb was so full of honey that it dripped. It would provide enough for some time to come!

He was in the act of lighting the extra grass when he heard a low growl from below. He looked to see what it was, and the strength seeped out of his legs, for directly under the comb was a leopard and it was climbing the rock to get him!

He tugged three times on the vine, but there was no response. Either Green and Ochella didn't feel it or they didn't have the power to pull him up.

Ndama waved the blazing grass at the bees hoping the fire would frighten the leopard and drive the bees into its face. But for some reason or other the leopard came on. He jerked the vine again, and again there was no response. Then he yelled, "Pull me up! Pull me up! There's a leopard down here!"

This time they pulled, but they pulled so hard the vine was cut in two on the sharp ledge of the rock! As he fell toward the approaching leopard he extended his arms and legs in an effort to brace himself on the walls of the stones. Fortunately there was a slight bulge in the stones in a place just above the leopard, and he managed to wedge himself there.

Without the protection of the fire he was now in a terrible plight. The leopard was so close he could touch it with his toes. The bees were humming viciously, stinging him where they could; and the leopard was advancing, its yellow fangs dripping with saliva. He knew that Bwana Green could shoot it with his gun, but to do so he'd have to climb down the rock and shoot it from below, and all this would take time.

Ndama prayed for wisdom to delay the leopard long

enough for the missionary to shoot it. Then, with a sudden inspiration, he grabbed a handful of honey and threw it into the leopard's face. The bees stung him as he did so, but he was so desperate he hardly felt them. The honey struck the leopard in the eyes. It opened its jaws and spat at him as he'd seen a tomcat spit at another in a midnight brawl.

He threw more honey at it, this time right down its throat. The leopard, blinded by the honey, jumped to the ground and tried to rub the sticky stuff out of its eyes by rolling around on the grass. This gave Green the necessary time to shoot it.

Ochella got the dead animal by the tail and pulled it out. Then Ndama jumped to the ground, got some more grass and smoked the bees from the comb. Green found a new vine and they let Ndama down. This time he filled the bucket with honey.

"Don't take it all," said Ochella.

"Why not?" asked Ndama.

"If you don't leave some for the honey bird it'll be angry and the next time instead of leading people to honey it will lead them to a sleepy rhino!"

The honey was good even though it was filled with eggs and dead bees. They gorged themselves on it. Ndama made some thin mud and spread it all over his stings.

As time went by the freshness of the spoor showed that the group was gaining on the elephant.

Green pointed to some broken shrubs. "By the looks of that," he said, "we may catch up with the elephant tomorrow. I only hope it's the rogue!"

They passed below a village, and when Ndama told one of the warriors what they were doing he replied, "Yesterday three big elephants went by. One of them was very, very big and it had a broken tusk."

Green tried to buy some vegetables from him, but the

man shook his head. Then he offered him the empty cartridge from the shell he had used to kill the leopard.

The man took it and rubbed it. Then he said, "I'll bring you some corn if you'll wait here."

"Do you think we ought to trust him?" asked Ochella. "You know that there are cannibals up here."

"He looked honest enough to me," said Ndama, rubbing his swollen hands.

A little later the man came back with an armful of roasting ears. "You see how the Lord provides," said Green, pulling back the husk on one of the ears and feeling the kernels. "The Lord always takes care of His own."

Ndama built a fire and roasted the corn on the spot. While they were eating it another villager ran up to them.

"Bwana," he said, gasping for breath, "I just came from a village on this side of the river. An elephant has been there. He's thrown the roofs off the houses and has killed thirteen cows. If you are a kind man you'll go and shoot it."

"When did you leave that village?" asked Green, getting to his feet and putting his gun over his shoulder.

"This morning, just as the sun was getting out of bed."

Green bit his lip. "That means that we are at least a day's journey away from it. And since it's getting dark now maybe we'd better stay here for the night and leave early in the morning."

"If you don't hurry," said the native, "it'll cross the river and you'll never get it."

"But we can't travel when it's dark," argued the missionary, sitting down and putting another ear of corn into the fire.

"Do as you please," said the man. "But please go after it as soon as you can. It has huge tusks and one of them has been broken off on the end. I saw the houses that he tramped down. They are as flat as the bottom of a river during a famine."

After he was gone Ochella said, "You know, I think this is all a trick. I think those fellows are cannibals and they want to eat us."

Ndama laughed. "You're worried about nothing," he said. "There's no doubt that the elephants have gone this way. How would this fellow know that we were looking for an elephant with a broken tusk? I believe he was telling the truth. But of course if they are cannibals they may try to eat us. But God has always helped us in the past and He'll help us now."

4 The River of Crocodiles

THEY were up ready to go just as the sun was getting out of bed. Leaving so early meant that they had to go on almost empty stomachs, for by this time the corn was gone and they were getting sick of honey. But they knew that the best time to rest was after they had killed the Rogue Elephant.

As they passed by various villages the people came out to stare, and when they learned they were on the trail of the elephant many of them smiled and wished them good luck.

At one village they found that the elephant had gone into their corn and had pulled up almost all of it. Everywhere people spoke of its enormous size and the fact that one of its tusks had been broken.

Green walked faster than the boys had ever seen him walk before. "Don't you think we should kill a deer and get something to eat before we go on?" asked Ochella.

The missionary shook his head. "I'm hungry, too," he explained. "But the elephant isn't far ahead, and if we keep right after it we may be able to kill it by tomorrow. Then we can get food to eat and return to Bunyore. Every day the rogue lives he causes that much more damage. The sooner we get him, the better."

"Well I hope we do pretty soon," commented

Ochella. "My stomach's so empty it's pressing against my backbone!"

The elephant's tracks were clearly visible in the soft ground, and they followed them without much trouble. But presently they came to a large sandy place. Here the tracks were almost invisible. Indeed, for a time they were so faint Ndama had to get down on his hands and knees to make sure they were following the proper tracks. Many other animals had wandered over the place and it was hard to tell the spoor of one animal from another.

Once while they were searching for the spoor Green said, "I hope when we find it we manage to shoot it in the proper place. Elephants are very hard to kill. Their skulls are so thick it takes a pretty large bullet to go through them and get to the brain. Those who are skilled in shooting elephants say there is a soft place right in the middle of their foreheads. If you shoot them in the head you must try and shoot them in this soft place. A while back a famous hunter shot an elephant on the slopes of Kilimanjaro. He had a heavy rifle, but the bullet struck it on the thick part of the skull. It failed to even knock it down. The elephant picked him up by the trunk, threw him into the air and caught him on his tusks. When the hunter's friends found him he had been tramped into little pieces.

"Let's pray that we don't have much trouble with this one. I'd hate to be killed before I've founded a few more missions for the Lord."

A wild boar suddenly charged by. And almost without thought Ndama fitted an arrow into his bow and shot. To hit a running boar, especially when one is unprepared, is a very difficult thing, but Ndama was a keen marksman and his arrow struck it in the hindquarters.

"It's too bad you didn't hit it in the heart," said Ochella.

"Don't worry, it'll be dead in a moment," replied

Ndama confidently. "That arrow was poisoned!"

The boar continued on, its tail straight up like a Masai spear, until it was out of sight.

"You didn't hit it hard enough," said Ochella.

"You don't have to hit an animal hard if your arrow is poisoned," replied Ndama. "All you have to do is to shoot the arrow in far enough to make it bleed. The poison on that arrow is a little old, but it's strong enough to kill it. You'd better start looking for firewood. When we get to the ridge over there you'll find a dead pig!"

The pig was dead just as Ndama had prophesied. He took a knife and quickly cut out a big piece of meat where the arrow had gone in and threw it away. Then he cut off the legs and skinned them.

"Do you really think we have time to eat now?" asked Green.

"Bwana Greeni, you are our leader and we'll do whatever you say," replied Ndama, "but I'm so hungry there's no strength in my legs. We can cook this meat in no time at all, and then we'll all feel a lot better."

The missionary didn't reply to this, but Ndama noticed that he went out and helped Ochella gather some firewood.

Ndama built a fire with bow and arrow as he had done the day before, then he cut some sharp sticks of wood to hold the pork as they roasted it.

"I hate to waste all the rest of the meat," said Ochella.

"I do, too," replied Ndama, "but it's the only thing we can do. If we could take the tusks back to Bunyore we could sell them, but there isn't time."

They roasted their meat in the fire and ate it with honey.

While Ochella and Green were finishing their meat Ndama dug a hole, cut the pig's head off and buried it. Then he piled some big rocks over the place.

"What's the reason for that?" asked Ochella.

"While we're gone the white ants will eat off the

meat," explained Ndama. "When we get back we'll dig it up, and there will be the tusks. I think I can sell them for enough to buy a pair of khaki shorts!"

Early on the following morning they knew they were quite close to the elephant because they passed a village where it had just torn up a dozen huts and killed several cows including a huge black bull. The inhabitants of the village who had the strength to do so fled into a nearby jungle. One of the older men who was lame and couldn't get away told them what had happened.

"We were all sitting on the ground eating boiled bananas," he said, a mixture of awe and terror in his voice. "Everything was just as usual when all at once someone started shouting, 'A mad elephant is coming!' I turned around to look, and there it was. Bwana White Man, when I saw how big it was my heart turned to water. Those who were able ran away as fast as they could. Because of my leg I couldn't run, so I hid behind a big rock. The elephant looked this way and that. Then it walked up to the houses and pulled the roofs off with its trunk and tossed them over its shoulder. Then it pushed the remaining walls over with its head and tramped them down with its feet. As it stamped its big feet on the ground the whole earth shook—just like it does during an earthquake. After it had done all of this it chased the cows and killed all that it could. I've seen lots of elephants, but this one is the meanest of them all. I think it's crazy. Bwana White Man, if you kill it with your thunderstick you will prove that you are a friend of the black people!"

"When did all this happen?" asked Green.

"It was just when the top of the sun came over the trees," replied the man earnestly.

"Then we'd better get on our way," said Green, leading on.

They walked as fast as they could. The villagers who met them on the way encouraged them to hurry, saying,

"It was moving very fast, and if you don't hurry it'll cross the river and you'll lose it because there isn't any bridge."

By noon Ndama and Ochella were worn out, but Bwana Green kept going. Ndama marveled at his energy. Then suddenly he stopped and put a hand to his ear. A shrill squeal filled the air.

"Did you hear that?" asked the missionary.

"What was it?" asked Ochella.

"I think it's the elephant," replied Ndama, squeezing his arm.

"From now on we must go carefully," said Green.

Ndama tossed some dry leaves in the air. The wind blew them in the direction from which they had come. "The wind's in our favor," he said. "But let's be careful and not make any noise."

They worked themselves up to a ridge that stretched out in front of them and cautiously peered over the top. A wide plain dotted with acacia trees was before them, and beyond that there was a long, deep valley.

Green filled the magazine of his rifle and tested the bolt action. "If I'm not mistaken," he said, "there's a river in that valley and we'd better get the elephant before it crosses because it's probably full of crocodiles."

Another squeal cut through the air. "That's the elephant all right," said Ndama, tightening his grip on his bow and arrows.

They hurried across the hot plains toward the valley. The squealing continued, leading them to a thick clump of trees that lined the river. As they approached the trees Green whispered, "We must be very careful. Remember this is a mean elephant. It would just as soon kill you as to take a drink of water. Let's be as quiet as possible, and above all stay behind me, and out of sight."

The trees were not as close together as it seemed from the distance. Ndama and Ochella followed as near to Green as they could. The elephant's trumpeting was now so loud Ndama's ears ached. He dodged from tree to tree, peering ahead, looking. Then Green waved for them to stop. Ndama fitted an arrow in his bow and waited. Green moved forward. Then he raised his gun to fire. Ndama tensed himself for the explosion, but there was none.

Instead there was a loud crashing ahead. He lifted his eyes and saw the elephant charging through the trees toward the river. Green followed it, but he didn't shoot.

Ndama pushed his way through the brush to Green's side. The elephant fled in front of them toward the river. As it approached the bank dozens of crocodiles that had been sunning themselves on the warm sand slid into the river. "Shoot it from here," urged Ndama.

"It would be no use," said Green. "I couldn't possibly kill it, and it would be terrible to just wound it and make it meaner than ever."

"What are we to do then?"

"The only thing I know is to wade across the river and get it on the other side!"

"But what about the crocodiles?" asked Ochella, his eyes wide with fear.

"We'll have to take that chance," replied Ndama, secretly enjoying Ochella's fright.

"Did you know that some of them are twenty feet long?" added Ochella, a shaky note in his voice.

The elephant plunged into the river and waded across.

"Now's the time to follow it," said Ndama. "The elephant's scared the crocodiles so much they'll leave us alone!"

"You can cross the river if you want to," said Ochella, "but I'm staying on this side!"

"While you're doing all this arguing the elephant is getting away," said Green, a little sharply. "You don't have to cross with me if you are afraid. But I'm going to cross. I'm not going back to Bunyore until I've killed the Rogue Elephant!"

"How are you going to cross?" asked Ochella.

"In the days of slavery," said Green, wiping the sweat from his face with a handkerchief, "the Arabs often crossed crocodile-filled rivers by shooting across them with their pistols. The noise scared the crocodiles away."

"It doesn't sound very safe to me," objected Ochella, glumly.

"Let's go," urged Ndama, "the gun will scare them off."

"All right," agreed Ochella, reluctantly, "but if a crocodile eats me it'll be your fault!"

They walked down to the bank, and then Green fired six shots over the water in rapid succession. Ndama held his bow and arrows over his head and led the way. The water was warm and the stones beneath his feet were uneven. But he didn't think about this. His eyes were on the opposite bank and a prayer that God would deliver them was racing through his head.

He had known people who had been eaten by crocodiles and he knew how treacherous they were. Once when he was out on Lake Victoria he pulled up a fish net. A long fish had been caught in the net. It had been bitten right in two by a crocodile–the crocodile's teeth had sheared it off as cleanly as any ax could have done.

He knew that a crocodile could swim under the water and bite their legs off the same way.

All at once something struck him. He jumped so quickly he fell under the water and his bow got wet. Then he saw that the object that had struck him was only a piece of wood! He frowned at it and continued on.

They were midstream when Ochella grabbed him by the shoulder. "Look!" he said, pointing with a shaky finger.

Ndama twisted his head and saw two sullen eyes staring at him from the water less than six feet away! The eyes were big and round and stupid. At first he was certain that it was a crocodile, and clammy sweat broke out all over his body. Then two nostrils appeared in front of the eyes. They were black and there were long, coarse whiskers between them. It was then he knew that the visitor was a hippopotamus. With this knowledge he began to inch his way forward to the opposite bank. Suddenly the hippo yawned, opened its mouth so wide he could easily have sat on the lower jaw without his head touching the roof of the upper jaw. The heavy eyeteeth, as large as big, peeled bananas, pointed right at him. Looking into its mouth was like peering into a red-painted cave. Ndama had heard that many a hippo had wrecked small boats with one enormous bite. He shuddered to think what would happen to them if the hippo decided to attack. He knew hippos ate grass, but one never knew when one of them would want to supplement its diet with a fat boy!

As he passed, the big pachyderm turned its eyes, following him. He tried not to look, but this was a difficult thing not to do. Suddenly the hippo sank under the water, disappearing without a ripple. Ndama's heart sank with it, for he wondered where it was going! He hurried on toward the bank. Then he stepped into a deep hole. As the water churned above his head he held his bow and arrows at arm's length to keep them dry. But the water was too deep. It seemed he would never touch bottom. Then something got him by the waist and pulled him up.

His ears roared. Then Bwana Green's voice broke through the noise, "Hurry! Hurry! A crocodile is after us!"

Without looking to see where the crocodile was coming from, Ndama made for the bank. Unfortunately he stumbled on a submerged rock and fell into the water. As he crawled to his feet he saw the crocodile behind him.

It was swimming rapidly toward him, its green snout just above the water and its eyes gleaming with the cold, cruel light of the jungle. The thick-skinned monster was about the same distance from him as he was from the bank. He plodded along as quickly as possible, skinning his knees and barking his shins on the moss-covered stones. But the crocodile was gaining all the time. In just a moment its horrible, tooth-lined jaws would open and he would be bitten in two!

In that brief moment he thought of his father at home, and how he'd be missed. He visualized his funeral being preached in Bunyore. He could hear the songs that would be sung in the crowded church, and see the tears on the black faces of his friends.

He fell down again, and this time when he looked the crocodile was less than a foot away!

Suddenly Ochella shouted, "Look out!"

Ndama ducked just in time to miss a heavy rock thrown by his brother. The rock struck the crocodile on the point of its snout. This stopped it for a moment–but just a moment. As it came on through the shallow water Ndama got a fleeting glimpse of its jaws. The lines were long and irregular. They had in them all the twists of a man who sneers at his mother, of one whose mind is diseased and who is on a murderous rampage. The heavy distorted lips that enclosed the foul teeth of the man-eating monster spelled, even in the fiendish language of the jungle, everything that is loathsome, cruel and horrible.

He churned through the water and grasped Ochella's hand, who by some miracle got to the bank first, and pulled himself up. At that moment Bwana Green fired. The bullet struck the crocodile in the eye, and a moment later it was kicking its feet at the bottom of the river, and a tiny crimson stream of blood was rising to the surface.

5 Cannibals

NDAMA staggered to the top of the bank and slumped in a heap like an empty bag. "I'm going to stay here until I get my breath," he muttered, clutching a bruised shin. "That crocodile was too close for me." He rested for a while. Then he said, "Did you see its teeth? They were as long as my finger—and there were hundreds of them!"

He was quiet for a long time, not a muscle moving. Then Ochella said, "If we don't hurry the elephant will get away."

"When you find the spoor I'll go with you," promised Ndama wearily, sitting up with a groan.

Green quickly located the spoor and started out. The muddy tracks led them up over the rim of the valley to a wide, grassy plain. But as wide as it was, the elephant was not in sight.

"It must be in a great hurry," commented Ndama, his eyes following the tree-lined horizon.

"A man at Nairobi told me that an elephant can go forty miles an hour for a short time," said Green. "But even if this fellow is ahead of us we'll catch up with him after awhile."

They plodded along, following the heavy tracks, the broken trees and the crushed grass.

Ochella pointed to some circling vultures ahead of them. "I wonder what's dead," he said.

"We'll find out when we get there. Maybe the Rogue Elephant has killed something," returned Ndama.

Soon they were in sight of a large village of neatly thatched huts. A man ran out to meet them, a heavy spear in his hand. "We want you to come to our village at once," he said excitedly. "An elephant just came and tore up some of the huts, and the chief is hurt. Bring some medicine and fix him."

The village was much bigger and much cleaner than the villages of the Masai. Their cone-shaped huts were well-constructed, looking much like those in the villages at Bunyore. As they stepped into the enclosure a little mongrel dog came out and snapped at them. Ndama tried to shoo it away, but when it refused to leave, and when the villagers merely stood around and laughed he fitted an arrow onto his bowstring and took careful aim. He didn't want to kill the dog, but also he didn't want to be bitten even though the dog was small. Finally the man who had invited them to the village said, "Don't shoot. I'll drive it away."

He whistled and threw a rock at its head. It ran off, its tail between its legs.

A quick survey of the damage showed that three huts had been tramped down and much of the grain in the nearby gardens destroyed.

"Tell them that we'd better get on our way so we can kill the elephant," said Green.

Ndama interpreted this into Swahili.

"There's no need to hurry," said a young man as calmly as one would say that it was going to rain. "The elephant will come back after a while. You can shoot it then."

"If we don't get it now it will tear up some more villages," said Green.

When Ndama interpreted this the natives exchanged curious glances with one another.

"I don't like this," whispered Ndama to Ochella. "These people are trying to play a trick on us."

"We want you to look at the chief before you go," said one of the younger men.

The chief was sitting in front of his hut, his leg doubled up under him.

"What happened to you?" asked Green kindly.

"The elephant caught me on its tusk," said the old man, a sharp groan escaping his lips.

Green stood his gun on the wall of the hut and carefully examined his leg. "I can't see anything wrong with it," he said. "It hasn't been cut and the bones aren't broken. There aren't even any bruises."

He turned his head toward Ochella, and then he gasped out loud, for the one who had invited them to the village was pointing the gun right into his face.

"Drop your bow and arrows," he said to Ndama, waving the muzzle of the gun at him.

"W-what is all this?" asked Green, flabbergasted.

The chief jumped to his feet and laughed. Then he said, "We have some things we want to talk over with you."

As Ndama listened to this he noticed that a group of armed warriors was surrounding them.

"Why are these men coming with spears?" asked Green.

"Because we don't want you to run away," said the chief, grinning until his yellow teeth reminded Ndama of the leopard that had almost gotten him when he was after the honey.

"You talk as if we were your enemies," said Green. "We're not enemies—we're your friends."

The chief eyed them sullenly. "I'm not a fool," he said. "My name is Dimbo. I'm the chief of the Gishu. I know when a man has caused me trouble!"

When he mentioned that he was the chief of the

Gishu, Ndama shuddered. He knew the Gishu were cannibals.

"We haven't done anything to harm you," argued Green.

Dimbo pointed to the ruined houses. "You did that and yet you say you're my friend. Those are the words of a snake."

"But we didn't do that," said Green. "That was done by the elephant."

"Don't say words of foolishness. The elephant ruined the houses, but you are the ones who sent the elephant."

"We were just trying to kill it. We can't help it because it came over here."

"I've heard hyenas laugh before. Your lies don't fool me."

"What are you going to do to us?" asked Ochella, his eyes bugging out.

"I don't know," replied the chief, fingering a long knife in front of him. "Our people are pretty hungry, and you look like you wouldn't be hard on the teeth." He felt his ribs with his hands. "You're not very fat, but I think you'd taste all right if we boiled you for a long time."

"Do y-y-you m-mean y-you are g-going to e-e-e-eat us?" asked Ndama, a quiver in his voice.

"Last year the locusts ate our corn," said Dimbo, sharpening the knife on the palm of his hand, "and so we ate the locusts. A year before that some rabbits ruined our gardens and so we made traps and caught the rabbits and ate them. And now you've driven an elephant into our village so that our property is ruined and the only thing we can do is to eat you."

"Is th-this supposed to be a f-funny story?" asked Ndama hopefully.

"No, it isn't a funny story," said the chief with a scowl. "We've been looking for someone to eat for a long time, and now you're here and we're going to take advantage of the opportunity."

The warriors advanced and tied each one of them up, binding their hands behind their backs. Then they placed them in a row in front of the chief's hut.

Dimbo tested the knots in the rope, and then he felt them all over, pinching them here and there to see where the best meat was. "I think this one here will be the best tasting," he said, pointing to Ochella.

"I don't think either one of us will taste good," said Ndama. "We're too thin and there's too much bone and gristle in our meat. Why don't you keep us here a while and feed us until we get fat. We'd be better eating then."

Dimbo shook his head. "That isn't a very good idea," he replied. "I have a lot of stomach trouble and greasy foods make me sick. I think I would rather eat you just as you are."

After the chief had gone Green said, "Boys, you must pray and ask God to help us. I knew that these people were cannibals, but I thought we'd kill the elephant before we got this far."

"I've been praying all the time," said Ochella.

Ndama watched as a dozen women put pots on their heads and marched out of the village. "They've gone to get water to boil us in," he said. "What do you think we can do?"

"Maybe we could break the ropes, or get them untied," suggested Ochella.

"They're too tight for that," replied Ndama.

"Well, then, maybe we could tell them that the government will punish them," said Ochella.

"These people aren't afraid of the government," put in Green.

"Maybe Bwana France will come to our rescue," said Ndama.

"I doubt it," returned the missionary. "He knows it takes a long time to track down an elephant. And, more than that, he's probably still sick."

Dimbo brought their conversation to an end. "We're

going to call in our friends from another village to help eat you," he said.

"When will your feast start?" asked Ndama.

"Today," replied the chief, rubbing his big stomach and licking his lips.

"If you eat us our friends will hear about it and will come and punish you," said Green.

"When they come we'll eat them, too."

"But they're wise people. They'll bring soldiers along with them."

"They may be wise, but they're not as wise as we are." He felt their flesh again and muttered mysteriously to himself.

"How are you going to cook us?" asked Ndama, stalling for time.

"Some of the people like their meat boiled, and some of them like it roasted, so we're going to cook you both ways."

"I think Ochella would taste better roasted," said Ndama.

Dimbo felt him all over again. "I think you're wrong," he said. "I'm a pretty good cook, and he's so tough I think he ought to be boiled. You're the one that should be roasted. We'll build a charcoal fire and roast you over that."

"How are you going to cook Bwana Greeni?"

The chief pursed his lips as he considered this. Finally, after thinking about it a long time, and after feeling his arms and legs and looking at him from different angles he said, "We've never eaten a white man before. Everyone will want a taste, and so I think we'll boil part of him and roast the rest."

"If you do all of this God will make you pay for it," said Green.

"Who is God?"

"God is the one who made the world and who made the people, and who sent His only Son to die for us."

"This is the first time I ever heard that, and I don't believe it. It can't be true."

"It is true even though you never heard it," continued Green earnestly. "God sees everything, and He'll see what you're doing. Why don't you untie us and let us teach you about Him?"

"The only thing I want to learn is how you taste," said Dimbo, rubbing his hands in anticipation. "One man said that he thinks you'll taste like crocodile meat. But I think you'll taste like rabbit."

Soon the women returned with the water, singing joyously as they walked along. Then they got three extra large pots and placed them on triangles of stones and filled them with water.

Next they built fires under them and placed plenty of firewood nearby.

When Dimbo came back Ndama, forcing his voice to remain calm, asked, "Are you going to boil us alive or are you going to kill us first?"

"We never boil people alive," replied the chief, shaking his head thoughtfully. "We always kill them first. But I think they taste better if we cook them right after we've cut their throats and their bodies are warm and quivering. And so we're going to let the water boil for a while. Then when our guests have all gathered we'll put in some salt and cook you. That way they can watch you cook and the delicious smell that comes from the pots will increase their appetite."

Soon the village began to fill up with the guests who had heard about the feast. Some of them came over and looked at the victims curiously, licking their lips when they felt their flesh.

Ndama watched them as they came in, and he was surprised by their number. It seemed to him that there were several hundred.

He kept twisting at the ropes around his wrists and legs, and praying that he would think of a way of escape.

Ochella had started to moan, and Bwana Green said, "Boys, we've come to the end. Let's die bravely, and let's pray that our death will be the means of sending out many more missionaries. Lots of missionaries have been killed and eaten, and I'm proud that I can suffer for the Lord."

"Don't give up so easily, Bwana Greeni," said Ndama. "The Lord is going to help me think of a plan."

"There's no use even trying to think of a plan, Ndama. We're doomed! If you got the ropes off where would you go? The warriors would spear you before you'd taken a dozen steps. But the Lord who saved us will take care of our souls. We have heaven to look forward to."

The crowd kept increasing. Then some drums were brought out and they began to dance. The fires under the pots were now burning full blast, and Ndama expected to hear the water boil at any moment. A Gishu warrior came over and felt their throats. Then he got a pair of knives and sharpened them on one another, hitting them together to the wild rhythm of the drums.

Suddenly the water in one of the pots frothed to the top. Immediately a woman pulled the firewood out a little and poured some salt into the water. Then another woman brought a mush paddle and stirred the water.

"Ndama, you've got to think of something," wailed Ochella, almost beside himself. "What will father do? We're his only boys! Ndama, this is terrible."

"I know it is, Ochella, and I'm trying to think of a plan, but I don't seem to think of one."

Another pot boiled over, and the woman took care of it as she had taken care of the first one.

"I never dreamed that I was going to be eaten by cannibals," said Ochella, straining at his knots until his biceps were like bands of steel.

"It won't do you any good to get the ropes off," said Ndama. "We've got to think of a better plan than that."

"Maybe we could tell them that we are poison and that they'll die if they eat us."

"That would be lying, and we're Christians. They wouldn't believe it anyway."

"I've got an idea," said Ochella, excitedly. "Let me roll over to the fire and hold the knot on my wrists in the flames. When the rope breaks in two I'll untie you, and then when the people get wild with their dancing we'll untie Bwana Greeni, and run off."

Ndama started to reply when some Gishu men came over to them. They picked them up and carried them to the center of the village. Then they returned and brought Green and placed him beside them.

6 Cannibal Soup

THE cannibals danced around them, grinning and showing their teeth and rubbing their stomachs. And each time they whirled by them one of their members stepped out of line and demonstrated to the victims how their throats would be cut.

"If you're going to think of a plan, you'd better think of one quick," said Ochella, his voice trembling like a banana leaf in a storm.

Suddenly the dancing stopped and Dimbo advanced toward them, a gleaming knife in each hand. He knelt by Ndama and carefully rubbed his neck, feeling for the jugular vein.

"I'm sorry that you're not going to be chief anymore," said Ndama, an idea suddenly coming to his mind.

"What do you mean?" demanded Dimbo, resting the blade of his knife on Ndama's throat.

"I mean that the people here won't like you any more."

"Why won't they?"

"Because you're stingy!"

"I'm not stingy. Look at all the people I've invited to eat. If I were stingy would I do that?"

"It's only a stingy man who invites people to his

village to eat and then sends them away hungry. After you've cooked us there won't be enough meat for half the people. They'll go away hungry and say that they should get a new chief because you're so stingy."

"There will be plenty of meat," said the chief. "I've eaten men before and I know how much is needed."

"I don't want to argue with you, Dimbo," replied Ndama, secretly praying with all his might, "but there won't be enough meat for even half the people. Look at Ochella over there. There's very little meat on him. He's so full of bone and gristle I'd rather eat a lizard's tail than him. His head is as hard as a rock, and I know it's solid bone. I know you're a good cook, but if you cook him it'll spoil your reputation."

Dimbo felt his thighs. "There's a lot of meat here," he said.

"I know there's some meat there," replied Ndama, "but that isn't enough to go around. And besides that his legs are awfully tough. You'd have to boil him a long, long time before you could eat him."

Dimbo thought this over for a moment. Then he said, "You have spoken words of wisdom, and so I've changed my mind. Instead of boiling you in big chunks I think I'll cut you up in little pieces and make soup out of you. I think both of you would make delicious soup!" He smacked his lips, enjoying the soup even before it was made. "And since there won't be enough meat to go around we can put some beans into the water and have bean soup. That kind of soup will be so good that when the people eat it they'll like it so much they'll say I'm the best chief who ever lived."

"Did you ever eat elephant trunk?" asked Ndama, desperately seeking for something to save him.

"A long time ago we caught an elephant in a pit, and I ate some of its trunk. It was very good," said the chief.

"I know it's good," said Ndama, forcing himself to

smack his lips. "Elephant meat is much better than human meat. A nice piece of elephant trunk boiled in beans would taste much, much better than Ochella. If I had an elephant here I'd cook you some and you would see for yourself."

"You've talked long enough now," said Dimbo, sharpening the blade of his knife on his palm. "The people are getting hungry and I think we'd better put you in the soup."

"Why don't you let us kill the elephant, and then have elephant soup?" asked Ndama. "If you had elephant soup there would be enough for everyone."

"I would do that, but the people are expecting to eat you, and you're here, and the elephant isn't. When a person gets his mind set on eating corn he hates to eat beans; and when he has it set on eating beans he hates to eat corn."

"Listen, Chief Dimbo," said Ndama, using his most flattering speech, and praying silently, "you don't know how good elephant trunk is. When we kill the elephant we'll cut off the trunk, and then we'll cut it into thick slices. Then we'll build a charcoal fire and cook it in the bottom of a wide pot. While it's cooking we'll put in some beans and corn and a little salt. If you cook us you'll find our meat is full of bones, but there are no bones in elephant trunk. Elephant trunk is really delicious. Just think how good it will be, taken hot from the fire with nice warm gravy all over it. There's no food in all your land as good as elephant trunk."

Dimbo listened carefully to this and Ndama saw that he was creating within him a hunger for elephant trunk.

"Did you ever smell elephant trunk when it's cooking?"

"I can't remember that I ever have."

"The smell is wonderful," said Ndama closing his eyes and smacking his lips. "When elephant trunk is cooked just right it just melts in your mouth, and the flavor lingers for a long time after you've eaten it."

"That sounds good," said Dimbo, "but I think we'd better eat you anyway. The people are getting terribly hungry and the water is boiling in the pots."

"But you haven't put the beans in yet," said Ndama, hoping to gain a few more minutes of life.

Dimbo ordered some beans put in the water and then he said, "Now we'll get you ready to put in."

"Before you prepare me for the soup let me tell you one more thing about elephant trunk," said Ndama, praying so earnestly the sweat came out all over his face. "If you could get some elephant trunk and feed it to your friends they would say that it's wonderful. I can taste it now. Mmmm, it's good. I wish I had some this very moment.

"And just think if you could kill the elephant you would not only have plenty of meat, but you would also have its skin to cut into narrow strips for rope."

"I wish we could kill an elephant," said an old man Ndama had not seen because he had been on the other side of him. "If you could kill it, it would help me a lot. I have rheumatism, and the best thing one can do for rheumatism is to kill an elephant and then to lay down inside it."

"My joints ache, too," said Dimbo. "Do you think that would help them?"

"It certainly would," replied the old man. "I was with some people who'd just killed an elephant. We took out its stomach, then I crawled inside and stayed about as long as it takes to milk a cow. The warmth of the elephant cured me quicker than a woman can spit!"

The dancers were becoming impatient. Some of them pointed to the victims and smacked their lips, hinting to Dimbo that it was time to start cooking them.

"Let's kill the elephant so you can cure your rheumatism," said Ndama anxiously.

"But what will the people say?" asked Dimbo. "They're hungry, I can't send them away without filling their stomachs. That would be impolite!"

"Do you want your rheumatism cured?"

"Ye-yes."

"Then untie us, and let us get the elephant."

Dimbo and the old man whispered together for a long time. Ndama prayed with all his might, and when he looked at Ochella and Bwana Green out of the corner of his eye he knew that they were praying, too.

The chief and the old man talked at length, then Dimbo motioned over some of his guests. Ndama watched their faces as they talked. And never before had he seen such angry looks. They looked like a starving man who had been given a plate of food, and then suddenly had it snatched away.

Dimbo turned to Ndama, "I'm sorry," he said, "but I'm afraid we'll have to eat you. They say they're so hungry they don't know what to do, and they are afraid if they don't eat you they won't have enough strength to go home."

"Tell them that if we are cooked there won't be enough meat to go around, but if we kill the elephant there'll be enough for everyone."

The chief repeated this, but they still scowled and shook their heads.

"Give us a chance," pleaded Ndama, on the verge of tears. "We want to give you plenty to eat, and if you'll give us a chance we'll kill the elephant and you can eat the trunk and crawl inside and let the warmth help your rheumatism."

Dimbo interpreted this. Then one of the men pointed to some circling vultures, and said something and laughed.

The chief laughed with him, holding his sides because of his mirth. When he got control of himself he wiped his eyes with the back of his hand and said, "We will give you a chance to live. The Gishu are very generous and we want you to know it. You had a bow and some arrows when you were captured. We're going to untie you and let you show us your skill as a marksman. You will be given three arrows and with these arrows you will have to shoot down two vultures!"

"Can I wait until they settle on a tree?" asked Ndama, hope beginning to return.

"No," said Dimbo, laughing and slapping his thighs. "You'll have to kill them while they're still flying."

"What will happen if I miss?"

"Then we'll put you in the soup!"

Ndama knew what a difficult thing this was. The vultures were flying at a good height, and it would be difficult to force an arrow up to them. And besides this there was a stiff wind blowing, and the wind changed directions from time to time. But it was a chance, and so he said, "Untie me, and I'll try it."

They removed the ropes and handed him three arrows. "Let me choose my own arrows," he said, noticing that those they had given him were not poisoned, and that two of them weren't quite straight.

"You'll have to use the arrows we gave you," replied Dimbo, winking widely at the armed warriors who stood by to see that Ndama didn't get away.

Ndama laid the bow and arrows on the ground. Then he rubbed his joints to get the blood to circulating properly, and prayed that God would help him.

He put an arrow on the string and waited for a vulture to fly over him. Soon one of them came, its dark wings extended, its eyes searching the ground. He drew back the string and let go.

The arrow whizzed up in the air, making a sound like a spitting cat. Ndama was confident that it would strike the vulture in the breast. But the horrible thing must have seen it coming, for suddenly it swerved to one side and the arrow missed.

The Gishu roared with laughter, and danced around rubbing their stomachs. And one of them tapped Ndama on the shoulder and pointed to the water bubbling in the biggest pot. Then he bit his arm and licked his chops and smacked his lips.

A moment later some of the younger cannibals joined hands and danced around the boys while they sang:

We'll cook you in the soup, yum, yum, yum,
We'll cook you in the soup, yum, yum, yum,
No elephant trunk for us, no, no, no,
We'll cook you in the soup, yum, yum.

Ndama prayed again, and put another arrow on the string. The shaft was bent, and he hated to use it; but there was nothing else to do. He waited until another vulture was in range and then pulled the string back to his ear and let go.

The arrow wobbled slightly as it left the sinew, but then it straightened out as it continued upwards. At first it seemed it would pass in front of the vulture. But this time his aim was just right and the arrow entered the scavenger's breast and it fell to the earth with a crash.

The Gishu warriors looked at one another as if they had seen a ghost. Then Dimbo said, "That was a fine shot, but you'll never do it again! You were just lucky."

Ndama picked up the remaining arrow and examined it carefully. There was a sharp bend in it between the metal head and the feathers. He hated to risk his life with it and so asked Dimbo if he might choose another.

The chief shook his head. "No, you'll have to use that one," he said with an evil grin. Then he joined the dancing circle of cannibals and added his voice to theirs in the horrible chorus.

Ndama bent the shaft in his hands, trying to straighten it out. Then he placed it on the bowstring and waited for another vulture. The vultures, now, however, were flying higher. Ndama hoped that one of them would come a little closer. But none of them did. Indeed the longer he waited the higher they flew.

Knowing that his chances to escape the soup were

rapidly slipping away he decided that he would shoot at the first one that came within range.

He glanced at Ochella and Bwana Green. He couldn't see them very well, but he knew that they were praying, and that he must not–must not–miss.

He looked at the feathers on the arrow, and noticed that one of them was loose. He knew that if the feather came off the arrow would swerve and miss. And he also knew that the feather might well come off when it passed over his hand that gripped the bow.

"I can see that I'm not going to miss my dinner," heckled one of the warriors in Swahili so that Ndama could understand.

"He'll never do it," yelled another.

"As soon as he shoots I'm going to yell and scare the vulture out of its course," put in another.

Ndama gritted his teeth and said nothing. Then a large vulture circled right in front of him. It was so high it seemed no larger than a sparrow. But he knew that this was his last chance and so he drew back the string, took careful aim and let go. He closed his eyes for he felt certain that he had missed.

But a moment later he opened them. The arrow flew higher and higher. He prayed that the vulture wouldn't see it in time to dodge. Then the arrow struck it in the chest. But instead of plummeting to the earth as had the other one it just circled around, losing ground all the time.

Ndama began to worry that it was merely wounded, and that after it had rested for a while it would fly off. But it circled to the earth and died right in front of them.

The Gishu stood around, their eyes wide, and their mouths open.

"Now you can let them loose," said Ndama, pointing to his brother and Bwana Green.

Dimbo picked up a knife and cut their ropes. He shook his head. "This is the most wonderful thing I've ever seen," he murmured. "But now what are the people going to eat?" As he said this a look of disappointment came into his face.

"Give me back my gun, and I'll get you something to eat," said Green.

The chief handed it over to him. Then he turned to his cannibal followers and told them that they'd have to go home. When this was translated to Green he said, "I don't want them to go home on empty stomachs. Have them stay. I'll go out and kill a kongoni and they can eat that."

"You mean you would do such a thing for us—your enemies?" asked Dimbo, his jaws hanging open in dumb surprise.

"Of course," answered Green, rubbing his wrists where the ropes had bitten into his flesh.

"I can't understand it," he replied, shaking his head.

"It's because we're Christians," said Green, motioning for some of the warriors to follow him.

Green didn't go far until he found a herd of kongoni. He shot three times, and killed three animals. The warriors who had accompanied him carried one of the kongoni in, and sent the others for the remaining two.

That afternoon the Gishu ate so much meat they could hardly walk. One man in particular ate and ate and Ndama wondered where it all went. Finally when he couldn't get any more down he said, "I'm sure glad I got to eat kongoni instead of Bwana Greeni. He doesn't look like he'd taste good at all!"

After the meat was gone Bwana Green preached to them and told them about Jesus Christ. The cannibals didn't understand much about the gospel, but they listened, and Ndama and Ochella were happy.

7 Rogues Are Mean

IMBO and the man with the rheumatism, who introduced himself as Jembe, accompanied Green and the boys on their way to get the elephant. The chief explained that he wanted to be on hand the moment the elephant was killed so that he could crawl inside while it was still warm.

The delay caused by the cannibals meant that the elephant was well ahead of them again. But there was distinct spoor to follow, and so they knew that they would catch up with it after a while. Much of Green's ammunition had been fired scaring the crocodiles and killing the kongoni, but he felt that there was enough to get the Rogue unless something drastic happened.

As they trudged along over the wide thorn-covered plain Ochella playfully poked Ndama in the ribs. "What did you mean by telling those people my head's as hard as a rock?" he asked.

"Isn't it?" replied Ndama innocently.

"You know it isn't!"

"I'll agree it's not as hard as a *hard* rock, but it's pretty hard and full of bone," put in Ndama. "Anyway, I saved your life and you ought to be happy. But I still think you'd be pretty tough and hard on the teeth."

"Do you suppose it does any good to lie down in an

elephant?" asked Ochella, stepping around some wait-a-bit thorns.

"I don't know. Bwana Greeni says the heat from the elephant's body might do some good. At least there would be no harm in it."

The hunters continued on until dark; then they made camp, built a fire and ate some of the kongoni they had brought along. They sat around the fire and talked for a long time, telling Dimbo and Jembe about the gospel. Then they piled on more wood and went to sleep by the fire.

Ndama and Ochella slept opposite the fire from the Gishu. "I still don't trust them," whispered Ndama.

"Bwana Greeni must not either, for he has his gun in his arms," said Ochella. "Maybe you'd better sleep for a while and I'll keep my eye on them. Then we can change about. You look so delicious they might be tempted to eat us."

The boys took turns at sleeping. Ndama especially found it hard to stay awake, but each time he closed his eyes he remembered how he'd just escaped the pot and this served to keep his eyes open.

Late in the afternoon Bwana Green stopped and put a finger to his lips. "Do you hear anything?" he asked.

Ndama put a hand to his ear and listened, then he tightened his grip on his bow for he heard the shrill trumpeting of an elephant coming from in front of them. "It's not far from here," he said.

"We must all be very careful," instructed Green. "This elephant is a mean one, and he'd love to kill us all. When we get up to it Ndama and I will go ahead while the rest of you scatter."

They followed the sound and were presently led into a thick concentration of acacia trees. Green and Ndama went ahead, their shoulders bent. Presently Ndama saw the dim outline of the beast. It was standing in back of a tall anthill with its tail toward them. Ndama touched Green on the shoulder and pointed to it, and waved to those behind to get out of the way.

The wind was blowing from them to the elephant. This put them to a disadvantage, and Ndama knew it. "Let's get around to its left side," whispered Green. "Maybe I can shoot it in the heart." They inched themselves around. But the elephant knew they were there for it began to nervously flap its big ears. Green put a fresh cartridge in the chamber of his gun, and pulled the hammer back. He checked to see that the safety catch was open. They crawled through the grass toward the anthill. The elephant curled its trunk and let out a terrible squeal, tramping its feet up and down like a soldier marking time.

"If we can get to the anthill without being seen we'll drop it without any trouble at all," whispered Green, leading the way.

The big pile of brown dirt put up by the ants was only fifteen or twenty feet away, but it seemed to Ndama that they would never get there. The elephant kept trumpeting and moving its ears as they approached. It sensed their presence, but couldn't make out just where they were. When they got to the hill they flattened themselves on the ground and gingerly peered over the top. Green rested his rifle on the top of the hill and took careful aim. But he was too late to fire.

The elephant suddenly located them, whirled and charged. Its trunk was curled in such a way it was impossible to shoot into the soft spot on its head. Its tusks were long and heavy, and the one that was broken was covered with black mud. Green fired and Ndama could hear the soft ker-whack of the bullet as it struck.

The big pachyderm took three or four steps forward and then fell, almost at their feet. Green took aim to fire again, but he wasn't quick enough. The elephant got to its feet and with one swing of its trunk threw Green a dozen yards away. Next it started after Ndama. He tried to run, but it did him no good. He felt the elephant's trunk as it wrapped around him and lifted him into the air. He knew this elephant was in the habit of holding people in its trunk and then tearing them to bits, on its tusks, and as he felt himself being lifted off the ground he hoped this wouldn't happen to him.

The Rogue held him in his trunk and looked at him for a long time, as if deciding what to do. Then it stuck him between its legs, and from that position tossed him in the air. As Ndama flew upwards he knew the elephant was going to catch him on its tusks when he fell. Fortunately, however, he landed on top of an acacia tree. The elephant waited and when he didn't come down it looked around until it discovered him in the tree. It rolled up its trunk and butted the tree with its head. The tree bent forward with its weight, and then snapped back, throwing Ndama away from it. He sailed through the air like a stone thrown from a sling, and fell on top of a thick clump of wait-a-bit thorns. These probably saved his life.

The elephant looked for him, stamping the ground angrily. But Ndama was so far away it didn't see him.

Green, however, was just a short distance off, and Ndama saw the elephant just as it located him. It started after him, its tusks lowered for a fatal thrust. But this time Green moved quickly and got behind a tree. The elephant butted the tree, and while it was busy doing this the missionary slipped over behind another tree. At a glance Ndama knew that there was only one way out of the situation and that was for him to kill the elephant himself.

Carefully he slipped through the grass, looking for his bow and arrows. He found the bow without much trouble, but the arrows were scattered around and it took a good deal of searching to find a poisoned one. By the time he found one and had it on the string ready to shoot, the elephant had almost broken the tree where Green was hiding. He took careful aim and let go. The arrow struck the Rogue squarely on the hindquarters.

The beast pivoted on its big feet, bellowed until the earth shook, and started for Ndama, its eyes blazing. Ndama dodged behind a tree and tried to hide himself in the grass. But the brute saw him, grabbed him in its trunk, shook him as a cat shakes a rat, and was in the act of tossing him again when an explosion filled the air. Ndama felt the wind rush by his head.

There was another explosion, and this time the big pachyderm went down completely. Ndama noticed the tiny hole in its forehead.

"We got it!" shouted Green, holding his gun high and waving it triumphantly.

In a few minutes Ochella and the Gishu were on hand to rejoice in the victory.

"If Ndama hadn't shot it with his arrow," said Green, "I could never have killed it."

Without a word Dimbo produced a knife. "Let's cut it open so I can crawl inside," he said with the eagerness of a small child.

Ndama found that opening up an elephant was a lot more difficult than opening a can of beans. The skin was thick and tough and they had to use an ax to cut through the ribs. And even after they had taken out the entrails it was hard to keep the abdominal cavity open. Finally Green kept it open by prying the ribs apart with a couple of stakes.

Dimbo, with a grin that seemed to circle his face a half dozen times, insisted that since he was the chief he should be the first one to get inside. Ndama and Ochella helped him climb up and jump in. Ndama waited until he had lain down and then he got a knife and proceeded to cut off the trunk.

The trunk was a lot thicker than he had thought it would be, and cutting it off wasn't an easy job. He got Ochella to help him, by twisting it this way and that. Unfortunately they twisted it the wrong way and the stakes slipped, causing the cavity to snap shut with a pop, locking Dimbo inside.

They opened it up as quickly as possible, and explained to the cannibal chief that it was an accident. He grumbled a bit about it, but he enjoyed being inside the elephant so much he presently lay down again and was very quiet.

When the trunk was off Green got the ax and started to cut away the flesh around the tusks. Ndama was surprised to discover how deeply imbedded the tusks were. Each time they chopped out some flesh they thought they would find the end, but each time they had to go deeper. Finally they came to the base of the roots and were able to pry them out.

Then Bwana Green gave a low whistle. "Look at this," he said, pointing to an old bullet that had lodged on the nerve of the broken tusk. He chipped it out and examined it carefully. "It looks like a slug from an old Arab gun. It must have been there a long, long time. Think of the pain the old boy must have suffered with that pressing against the nerve all these years. No wonder he became a rogue! That's the way sin spoils people's lives. It causes them to do all kinds of things. The only thing that can cure sin is the precious blood of Jesus Christ."

Dimbo climbed out of the elephant and sat on the ground while Jembe took his place. "Do you feel any better?" asked Ndama.

"Much better," replied the old man, grinning. "I feel better than I've felt for a long, long time."

Pretty soon Gishu began to pour into the place. How they knew the elephant was dead was a mystery. They brought knives along and soon were cutting off great slabs of meat. Some of this they put away and some of it they ate raw. Ndama cut off several slices of trunk and cooked it over a fire Ochella had built. Jembe stayed in the elephant until all the meat was cut off. When he got out he said he felt better than he'd ever felt in his whole life.

As soon as the sliced elephant trunk was ready Ndama invited Dimbo to join them. Bwana Green said the blessing and they started to eat. Dimbo smacked his lips as he chewed. Ndama noticed a faraway look in his eyes, and he wondered if the cannibal chief would rather have eaten them.

"Is it good?" he asked.

Dimbo grinned. "It's very good."

They ate elephant trunk until they couldn't hold any more. Green took out the Gospel of John and motioned for the cannibals to gather around. The Gishu formed a circle and watched him curiously, some of them eating meat, and others holding big chunks of it in their hands.

"We are very glad we killed the elephant," said the missionary. "We are happy that it won't kill any more people or cattle or destroy any more houses, and we are happy to have met you. And now I want to tell you about Jesus Christ, and how He came to this earth and died for us on a cross."

The cannibals listened quietly to everything he said. Then Dimbo got to his feet. "What you have said about Jesu Christo is very interesting, but we can't understand it," he said.

Green told them the story again, and this time he emphasized the fact of sin and how it binds people. It was hard to get this across to them, but they nodded their heads while he talked. "Do you have any thieves in your country?" he asked.

"We have many," answered Dimbo.

"What do you do to them?"

"We burn their hands so that everyone can see the scars."

"Does that stop them from stealing?"

"No, it doesn't."

"The reason they can't stop stealing is because stealing is in their hearts. When a person confesses his sins to Jesus Christ He not only forgives their sins, but He changes their hearts as well.”

After Green had taught them a while, he said, “I wish some of you would help us carry the tusks back to Kitale.”

Dimbo pointed to a dozen men and told them to pick up the tusks and follow Green to their village.

The tusks were carried to Dimbo’s village. Here Green and the boys rested for a whole week, and held services for the Gishu. The cannibals listened each day as the missionary taught them about the Bible and the way of salvation.

At the end of one of the services Jembe stood up and said, “We’ve enjoyed listening to all you’ve had to say, but I can’t understand why it’s wrong to eat people. I might agree that it’s bad to kill someone to eat, but I can’t see anything wrong in eating a person who was killed in an accident or by a wild animal. You people ate part of the elephant. What is the difference between eating an elephant and a man? The only difference I can see is that the man talked and the elephant didn’t.”

“The difference between eating a man and an elephant,” explained Green, “is that a man has a soul, and an elephant doesn’t.”

The Gishu didn’t understand this, and so Green took a whole day to teach them how man was made in the image of God, and how he has a soul that never dies.

The cannibals listened to this with great interest, and some of them seemed to understand.

At the end of each day Dimbo had a large pot of sweet potatoes cooked for his guests, and as they ate he asked question after question. “Where is God?” he asked. “Why did He have a son? Why did He let men kill Him when He had all power? Can black people be saved? Do snakes have souls? Can God forgive murder? Is it wrong to beat your wife? Will women go to heaven?”

Green answered all the questions he could, as foolish as some of them were.

The day before they were to leave his village Ndama went over to Green and said, "How are we going to carry the tusks back to Kitale and how are we to cross the river. I don't want those crocodiles to have another chance at me."

"Maybe the Gishu will help us," said Green, leading the way over to Dimbo and some of his friends who were talking in front of his hut.

"The ivory is heavy," he said to the chief. "We can't possibly carry it to Kitale by ourselves. We were wondering if some of your people would help us."

Dimbo scratched his head and spoke to his friends in low whispers for a long time. Then he said, "We'll help you get across the river, but we won't go any farther."

"We are glad that you will take us that far," replied Green with a smile. "But how will we get the tusks to Kitale if you don't help us?"

"We would take you the full way, but if we go into the land of our enemies they might eat us," replied the chief.

"Nonsense! No one would want to eat you," replied Green, forcing himself to laugh.

"You, you mean you don't think I'm fit to eat!" replied Dimbo angrily.

"N-no, I-I didn't mean that," apologized Green. "I just meant that the people there don't eat human beings, and I'm sure they wouldn't eat you or any of your friends. People who believe in Jesus believe that each person is worth more than all the world."

The chief motioned his friends a little closer and began to whisper again. And by the earnestness of their faces Ndama knew the subject they were discussing was very serious.

8 Grinning Cannibals

F WE GO with you to Kitale," said Dimbo, "you may get all of your white friends to surround us and tie us up, and even if you don't eat us you'll keep us from returning home."

"We'd never think of such a thing," returned Green. "If we were your enemies we'd have shot you with our gun a long time ago. And besides that, didn't we kill some kongoni for you? If we had been your enemies we'd never have done anything like that. We're followers of Jesus Christ, and He taught us to return good for evil. If I had been your enemy I would have left you inside the elephant, and you would have died there."

The chief whispered with his friends again, and then he said, "You have spoken words of wisdom, and I'm going to send some men with you. If they don't come back we'll know you've eaten them. And if this happens and another white man comes to our country we'll eat him quicker than a woman can spit!"

A dozen Gishu warriors, armed with razor-sharp spears, joined Green and the boys as Dimbo led them to the river. When Ndama mentioned to one of them that he was worried about crossing the stream the warrior replied, "We'll get you across all right. Don't worry about it."

The banks of the river this time were simply covered with slumbering crocodiles sunning themselves. There had been no charging elephant to chase them into the river. They looked like so many logs on their way to a mill. Ndama estimated that there must have been at least fifty of them.

Green went ahead and by firing quickly shot three of them before they could escape into the water.

"Now, how are we going to cross?" asked Ndama.

Instead of answering, Dimbo ordered his men to make two large piles of rocks. Then he asked Green to shoot over the water and for his men to throw the rocks in, one pile to be thrown in on one side of a narrow corridor, and the other pile to be tossed in on the other side. While this was being done he stepped into the water and boldly walked across, with Ndama and Ochella and half his men following. On the other side he had his men gather more rocks and throw them in while the others crossed.

"That's a very dangerous river," he explained. "A short time ago a man and his wife were seized by a monster crocodile when they were in the middle of the stream. It bit them in two just like that!" He snapped his fingers to emphasize what he meant.

"How will you cross it on the way back?" asked Green.

"We'll just throw in a lot more stones," he replied with a grin.

When it was time to make camp Green shot a kongoni and Dimbo and his men dressed it while Ndama and Ochella gathered wood and built a fire. They roasted the meat on the hot coals, and Green preached to them again. After he'd finished his sermon Dimbo got up and said, "I still don't understand much about what you are saying. But I'm beginning to believe that the words you say are true words. The reason I believe this is because Bwana Greeni is so kind to us. He has a thunderstick with him and it is very powerful. It makes so much noise it kills anything he points it at. He killed this kongoni when it was a long way off. He could kill us if he wanted to. But he doesn't. We did him much harm when we decided to eat him. But instead of returning bad for bad and evil for evil he returns good for evil. I never met anyone like him before. I want him to tell us why he does this."

Dimbo sat down and the Gishu nodded their heads to indicate that they agreed to all that he said, and that he was speaking for them.

"The reason I give good for evil is because I am a follower of Jesus," said Green. "Before I followed Him I returned evil for evil and I hated my enemies. But after I believed that He died for me He gave me a new heart, and now I love my enemies."

"Could this Jesus you speak about give us new hearts even though our skins are black?" asked Dimbo.

"He'll give anyone a new heart who'll do what He says and believe on Him."

"Would He give me a new heart?"

"If you'll do what He asks you to do."

"If He will, I want a new heart, and I want a new heart right now."

Green showed him the way of salvation, explaining each part, and the cannibal chief got on his knees and asked God to save him. When he got up there was a glow on his face and he said, "I feel wonderful inside. Everything seems so different. The grass is nicer and the sky is more beautiful, and I—and I love my enemies. Oh, it's wonderful!"

Dimbo then turned to his men and instructed them how to find "the peace that passeth understanding." Three of them believed immediately. Green told them that they should all be baptized, and that as soon as they found a small river where there were no crocodiles he would baptize them.

The next day they found a clear stream that was so small there were no crocodiles or hippos in it. Here the missionary baptized them. Those who were baptized said that they were happier than they had ever been in all their lives.

Ndama and Ochella taught them how to sing some hymns in Swahili. They enjoyed the songs immensely and sang together as they carried the elephant tusks on to Kitale.

On the last day of the journey Dimbo said, "I'm certainly glad you came to our village, and I'm glad that you taught me about this new religion. But now that you'll be gone who will there be to teach us? We would like to have a white man live in our village who would teach us more about God and about the things that are in the book you read."

"I'll try and have one sent," said Green. "But I don't know how soon it will be."

When the chief was out of hearing distance Green walked up to Ndama and said. "The chief's words have made me sad. I wish I could have a missionary sent to them right away. But I got a letter from our Missionary Board a while back and it said that they were short of funds; that it was all they could do to keep what missionaries they have on the field.

"And the pitiful thing is that there are hundreds of places in Africa and India and other parts of the world where the people want missionaries but there is no money to send them. If the people in America and other Christian nations could really see the need they would send out more missionaries. I'm going to write a story about Dimbo and how the cannibals almost ate us. I hope that the boys and girls in America who read the story will be stirred up to give money to support mission work. And better still, I hope some of them will listen to the Lord and if He calls them to the mission field they will be willing to go."

Suddenly Ndama stopped and snapped his fingers. "We forgot something," he said.

"What was it?" asked Ochella.

"We forgot to dig up the hippo's skull. I wanted to sell the tusks to get money to buy a new pair of pants!"

"Don't worry about that," said Green. "I'll buy you a new pair when we get to Kitale."

The game warden was very happy when the tusks were brought in. He looked at them carefully to see how good the ivory was. Then he weighed them. The one that was broken weighed ninety-five pounds, and the other tipped the scales at just over one hundred.

"You did a fine piece of work, Bwana Green," he said, rubbing his hands together to show his enthusiasm.

"I don't deserve the credit at all," replied the missionary modestly. "If it hadn't been for Ndama and Ochella we'd never have gotten back." Green then told him about the cannibals.

"I can talk to the chief of police and have some soldiers sent over and arrest them," offered the warden.

"No, we don't want you to do that," said Green. "Dimbo has become a Christian."

"You mean he's converted!" exclaimed France.

Green nodded, "Yes, he and several of his friends surrendered themselves to Jesus Christ, and have reformed."

"I'm glad to hear it," replied the warden, his eyes a little misty. "A long time ago I learned that the only one who can change a man's life is Jesus Christ. Locking people up doesn't change them, it just keeps them out of mischief while they're in jail. The missionaries have done more good for Africa than anyone else!"

When the time came for the missionary and the brothers to leave for Bunyore, Dimbo approached them with tears. "Please, Bwana Greeni," he pled, "please come and stay with us for a while and teach us about God."

"I'd love to," replied Green, "but I have a school back at Bunyore and I have to return. But I'll write to our land and tell them of your need, and maybe a missionary will be sent to you."

9 Conclusion

NDAMA and Ochella climbed into the lorry with heavy hearts. They had nearly lost their lives in the land of the cannibals, but now that it was over they enjoyed the memory of the excitement and the pleasure they would have in relating their experiences to their friends.

There was a great throng of people at Bunyore to greet them, for by some way or another the news of their arrival had gone on ahead. In their hurry to get home Ndama had failed to get his new pants, and so during much of the greeting he had to sit in the cab of the lorry. But Ochella had stuck them together with thorns, and they weren't too bad.

The Bunyories prepared a great feast, and when Bwana Green saw that they were going to butcher a cow to celebrate their return he took the opportunity to drive Ndama to Luanda and buy him three pairs of new red pants.

There was plenty of obusuma at the feast, and Ndama and Ochella had all the beef they could hold. But Ndama was disappointed because there were no locusts, and when no one was listening he whispered to Ochella, "I think elephant trunk tastes a lot better than cow meat. It has a stronger flavor!"

After everyone had eaten, one of the elders got to his feet and said, "We are glad that Bwana Greeni and the brothers are back. We were a little worried for a while, because we knew they had gone to get the Rogue Elephant. It is our hope that they will never have to risk their lives again.

"We are all proud of Ndama and Ochella, proud that they are Christians, and proud that they are afraid of nothing; not even lions, crocodiles or cannibals. We hope that when they grow up they will become preachers and preach to us the story of Jesus. And to show how much we appreciate them we have brought them a present."

He presented a brown package to each one of them. Then someone in the crowd shouted, "Open them up. Let us see what you received."

With trembling fingers the boys cut the sisal string that bound their gifts. And then they laughed. For in each package there were three pairs of red pants!

The Bunyories examined the pants and declared that they were the best ones they had ever seen. And one man said, "I hope these new ones won't be ripped by a rhino's horn, because I gave all the eggs my old hen laid to help pay for them!"

Just then a runner rushed up to them shouting: "There's a great big snake in our village. It's so big it has already eaten three goats. If you love us you'll come and kill it. But anyone who comes will be risking his life because it's as big around as a tree and it's twice as long as Bwana Greeni's lorry!"

Ndama grabbed his bow and arrows. "Let's go after it," he said, taking Ochella by the shoulder and following the runner.

Man-Eaters Don't Laugh

PART II

A Missionary Adventure Story

BY CHARLES LUDWIG

1 The Warning Message

NDAMA rubbed the sleep from his eyes, and then cautiously opened the crude wooden door of their hut. The soft thump that had awakened him was so different from the sound of an ordinary knock–and the difference frightened him. He peered out into the star-studded night. Then he sucked in his breath with a start, for an arrow was quivering in the door; and on the smooth brown shaft, just below the feathers, was a note, tied in place with a piece of sisal string!

With trembling fingers he twisted the arrow from the wood, closed and bolted the door. Christian friends at Bunyore had warned them that anything might happen at Kisumu. Ndama knew that this was true, for Kisumu, a port on Lake Victoria, was a hotbed of savage terrorism. But Bwana Green had needed him, so he and Ochella had come at the risk of their lives.

He reached out his hand on the floor and shook his younger brother awake.

"What do you w-want?" asked Ochella, creeping deeper under the red cotton blanket.

"Look at this!" whispered Ndama as he unfolded the note by the fire.

He spread the stained wrapping paper out in his hands and tried to read it, but there was not enough light to make out the pencil-scrawled words. Ochella pulled a handful of grass from the roof and thrust it into the smoldering coals. Then he knelt on the floor and blew until the grass burst into flames.

As the small room lit up Ndama exclaimed excitedly, "Listen to what it says! 'We're coming to get you at midnight. You must take the oath and help drive the white man from Africa. Death follows those who refuse!'"

The grass had burned too low for him to follow the signature. He pulled some more grass from the roof and pushed it into the coals. When it flared up enough for him to read, he added, "The note is signed, 'Dando.'"

"It's eleven-thirty now," put in Ochella nervously. "Maybe we'd have time to escape. The police at the station would–"

"We'd never get there," snapped Ndama. "Our hut is probably surrounded by Luo!"

Ochella opened the door a few inches and the loud crack of a crocodile letting its jaws snap together drifted in from the nearby lake.

The boy had barely closed the door when he heard a heavy knock and a harsh voice demanding, "Are you ready?"

Ochella noisily slipped the bolt into place.

"You'd better come out," warned the voice. "We have matches and we'll set fire to the roof if you don't!"

"Wh-what'll we do?" stammered Ochella in a loud whisper.

"All we can do is pray. We–"

"Open the door!" thundered the voice.

Ndama and Ochella sank to their knees and closed their eyes. With a quivering voice Ndama prayed, "Dear God, You helped us when we were seized by the cannibals in the land of the Rogue Elephant, and we know that You can help us now."

"*Unlock the door*, I said!" screamed the voice, now edged with anger. "If you don't open it we'll burn you out.

I'm going to strike a match, and if you don't come out by the time I count six I'll touch it to the roof. You'll be burned like locusts." The Swahili words rang out, "*Moja–mbili–tatu–nne-tano*–I'm warning you! If you're not out when I say six you'll be roasted alive!"

Just as the savage was saying six, Ndama opened the door and bravely stepped out into the night. Ochella followed closely behind. A tall Luo, wearing a goatskin, faced them. "It is good you opened the door," he said in crude Swahili. "If you had not you would have gone up in smoke. The Luo are very impatient, especially with boys who work for missionaries!"

He glanced inside the empty hut. Then he said, "This evening you will have the great privilege of taking the secret Luo oath." He pointed with his spear to a path that skirted the lake. "This is the way we'll go," he commanded. "You are going to be highly honored in being allowed to take the oath from Dando–the most powerful of all our witch doctors. No one would dare break the oath after they've received it from him!"

"But we don't want to take it," said Ndama.

"Don't utter the words of an infant," replied the man sullenly. "If you join our society you can return to your land and give the oath to others. And then the white people will be driven from our country and you'll have a good chance to be a chief."

"I don't want to be a chief," replied Ndama promptly. "My chief is Jesu Christo, and I want to do His will more than anything else."

Soon three other Luo joined them. They were armed with petal-shaped spears and dressed in goatskins like the leader.

"You are wasting your time," continued Ndama, speaking loud enough for all to hear. "We are Christians and we'll never take your silly oath. Never! Never! Never!"

The one who had knocked at the door stopped, and

pushing his face right up to Ndama's exclaimed, "My name is Thuku. I'm a big man around here. Everyone knows that I'm the toughest and the meanest of all the Luo. No one refuses to take the oath when I'm around. At least they don't refuse anymore, for everyone knows better now. The seven who refused a while back were fed to the crocodiles. You should have seen the terror on their faces when we threw them into the lake! I'm—"

"You are just a murderer," cut in Ndama crisply, after he had stepped back in order to avoid the man's foul breath. "It doesn't take courage to throw people into the lake. That's what cowards do. Men with real courage accept Jesu Christo and serve Him!"

"Keep still!" ordered Thuku. "I don't want to hear that kind of talk. I will never become a Christian. Never! Christians are all cowards!"

"If you think they're cowards you should travel with us," said Ndama. "Christians are the bravest people in the world."

"Come on out of the house," insisted Thuku.

"But we're not about to take your silly oath," returned Ndama, refusing to budge.

"We'll see about that," snapped Thuku, striking him viciously on the cheek. Then he prodded him with the lower end of his spear and ordered him and Ochella to march.

The boys followed a narrow path that wound through thick clumps of tall papyrus, slender eucalyptus trees, and dense patches of jungle. A full moon lit their way and cast eerie shadows into the unknown around them.

Suddenly the path dipped into a shallow beach skirted with a light undergrowth. A dozen huge crocodiles were lying on the beach, each one in an excellent position to slide into the water at a moment's notice.

"They are my friends," said Thuku. "And the reason they are my friends is that sometimes I provide them with extra food." He tossed a stone into the lake, and several of the crocodiles slid into the water. "See, they are ready to obey my every wish," he continued with a sidelong glance at Ndama.

"If you're trying to scare me," said Ndama, "you are wasting your time. I am a follower of Jesu Christo, and He will help me through any difficulty. My trust is in Him!"

Thuku's only answer to this was a sneering laugh.

There were a half dozen men at Dando's hut who had come to take the oath. Four of them had come willingly. Two of them had been forced.

The witch doctor was sitting on a small three-legged stool in front of his mud-and-wattle hut. There were wide streaks of white mud on his cheeks and a grisly spinal column around his short, thick neck. Three or four necklaces of cowrie shells hung loosely on his black chest, and the wooden handles of several small knives protruded from the greasy belt around his heavy waist.

A fire of driftwood sputtered a few feet away, and the light flickered on the old man's face.

He stood up and grinned at them, revealing almost toothless gums. "And so you've come to take the oath that will drive the white man from our land," he began eagerly.

He hacked loudly and spat on the ground in front of his clients. Then he got a dozen fresh banana leaves and sprinkled blood on them, from a mysterious-looking black pot. Next he placed the leaves in the door of his hut. "Those who are to take the oath will step over the leaves and enter," he said with a dramatic sweep of his arms.

The volunteers bent low because of the short door and solemnly stepped over the blood-sprinkled leaves.

When it was time for Ndama and Ochella to go in they stoutly refused. "I will never enter," said Ndama bravely.

"Then you are an enemy of the black people," retorted the witch doctor.

"I'm no one's enemy," returned Ndama heatedly. "But I know that the only way to help our people is through Jesu Christo–and not with this method of fire and murder–"

Dando's mouth sagged with unbelief. "Do you know who I am?" he demanded with a swagger.

Ndama and Ochella were silent.

"Do you?" shouted the medicine man, scowling until his black face was hideous.

"Yes, I know you are a witch doctor, and that you force people to take horrible oaths," returned Ndama wearily.

Thuku grabbed the brothers by their necks and roughly pushed them inside. "This is not a game," he snapped as they stumbled through the door. "If you try any more nonsense I'll use a club!"

It was dark in the hut, for there was no chimney to let the smoke escape from the fire in the center of the floor.

With great solemnity the witch doctor took his place behind a small arch of tree limbs. Then he asked each candidate to kneel in front of him, starting with the oldest. In a low monotone he said to the first one, "Repeat my words and mean them with all your heart."

The kneeling man nodded, agreeing that he would comply.

"I will not accept the religion of the white man," began the witch doctor in a singsong chant that gurgled from his throat like bubbling obusela. "If I do this oath will kill me.

"I will defend everyone who is against the white man.

"Anyone who is against the white man is my friend even though he is a Bunyore, a Masai, or a Swahili.

"If I am called in the middle of the night to burn a white man's house I will do it.

"I will never pay taxes to the government even though I have to rot in the Kisumu jail."

As each man repeated these terrible words beads of sweat came on their faces and streamed down their backs.

Dando then poured some blood into a small yellow gourd. He flexed his fingers like the outstretched claws of a leopard, and then waved them over the foaming blood and mumbled magic words. While he did this there was absolute quiet in the hut. The Luo barely breathed as they followed his every move with their large awe-filled eyes.

The men swallowed the blood greedily, and stepped out into the darkness.

When it was time for Ndama and Ochella to take the oath they flatly refused.

Thuku pled with them. Getting no place, he angrily boxed their ears.

"Don't do that," cautioned Dando. "They refuse to take the oath because they don't know what we are doing. If they knew how the foreigners had taken our land they would believe in us and take the oath." He then went on to explain the grievances the Luo had against the whites.

"Bwana Green isn't like that," argued Ndama boldly. "He's a missionary. He preaches the gospel. I was saved because of his instructions."

"White men are white men," retorted Thuku after he'd slapped them again.

"Even if they were all bad this is not the way to help them," said Ndama.

"The only way to get them to leave our land," replied Thuku, "is to burn their houses, laugh at their religion and–and cut off their heads!"

When Ndama and Ochella still refused to be persuaded Dando took them outside. He led them to a scaffold made of sisal poles with a rope dangling from the crossbar. "If you don't take the oath right away," he threatened, a grim mock in his voice, "we'll suspend you from the rope and build a slow fire under your feet!"

"Yes, I've heard what you do," replied Ndama, praying silently. "I know how you tortured Josephu, the pastor of the Lando church. But he didn't give in. You killed him and now he's in heaven." Ndama pointed to the stars. "Your silly oaths will never stop the work of Jesu Christo. He is the Leader of leaders; the Chief of chiefs; the only Son of God!"

Ndama looked him right in the eye for a long moment, and then added, "Thuku told me you are the most powerful witch doctor here. Is that true?"

"It most certainly is," answered the medicine man.

"They say you can kill people with magic. Is that so?"

"Yes, it is true. I could say magic words that would kill you right now."

"Are you sure?"

"I most certainly am."

"You're talking baby talk," replied Ndama, marvelling at his own courage. "Your words are as empty as those of a crocodile's grandmother. When I was in the land of the Masai, their most famous witch doctor tried to kill me with magic, but he couldn't. Neither can you!"

Thuku raised his spear, threatening to run him through. Ndama, however, merely gritted his teeth and paid no attention. He took the Gospel of John from his khaki trousers and flipped the white pages. "This book is full of powerful words, for these are the words of God. They can change a man's life–" As he pointed to the various pages he spoke calmly even though Thuku was so angry his eyes blazed.

"My words are powerful!" hissed Dando, his eyes protruding from his evil face until he resembled a toad. "I could kill you this very moment if I chose."

"Why don't you?" asked Ndama.

"All right," screamed the old man trembling with rage, *"I will!"*

He waved his bloodstained fingers in front of the boys
and mumbled several groups of words. When nothing
happened and they continued to smile he licked his thick
lips, spat on the ground and mumbled some more. The
effect on the Luo was immediate. They stepped back as if
they were afraid the magic might accidentally kill them.

The medicine man repeated the words again and again,
but nothing happened.

The Luo, curious that the boys still lived, stepped
closer.

"The reason Thuku and some of these others act as
they do," said Ndama calmly, "is because you forced them
to take this childish oath, and they are afraid the oath
will kill them."

He turned to Thuku. "You are good beneath your
anger," he continued, his voice still as calm as the bark of
a tree. "You learned to read and write from a missionary.
I know. Someone told me about it. But you are afraid
because you took this silly oath. Is that not so?"

Thuku stared at him silently. His face was as
motionless as a granite boulder.

"What I said is true, is it not?" persisted Ndama.

Slowly the cruelty drained from Thuku's face and
he nodded his head.

"You were forced to take the oath, weren't you?"

"Y-yes, I w-was," he murmured slowly.

There was a heavy silence in the circle of Luo as
Ndama went on. "You would like to behave yourself again,
wouldn't you?"

Thuku nodded his head.

"There is a way for you," said Ndama. "This oath
you have taken has no power. Jesu Christo has much
power and He will change your heart and make you a
new person if you'll let Him. Turn to Him. He wants to
save you!"

Thuku hesitated for a moment, his eyes moving from
one Luo to another. And then, while they rested on the face

of Dando, he said, "Ndama is right. From this day on I'm going to follow Jesu Christo. I know how He changed the lives of my parents, for they heard the story of Jesu from the first missionary who came to Kisumu. I know His way is the right way."

"Do you know what you are saying?" demanded the witch doctor as he fingered the spinal column around his neck.

"I do. I have been thinking about these things for many days."

The witch doctor ran his tongue over his lips. Then his face tightened with cruelty while he said, "I'm going to give you until this time tomorrow to change your mind. If you don't you know what will happen–Asila, here, will help me carry out the justice of the Luo. My words didn't kill these two boys, but at home I have a medicine, the most powerful medicine that ever was, and I'll use that on them. They'll wish they never heard of this Jesu Christo!"

Asila stepped out of the crowd and swaggered up to Ndama and Ochella. "I don't think you know how powerful Dando is," he said importantly. "You probably think he is about like some of the witch doctors up in Bunyore.

"No, Dando is not like them. He is the most powerful witch doctor in the whole world. By saying a magic word he can put a pair of shoes in a man's stomach! That is true, isn't it?" he asked, turning to the crowd for confirmation.

"Kweli, Kweli! (Truly! Truly!)" replied the people with one voice.

"When Dando uses the medicine he has at home your blood will turn into water, and your heads will be filled with lizards," continued Asila. "That's true, isn't it?" he asked again.

"Kweli! Kweli!" chanted the crowd, their voices even more united.

"Last week a man refused to take the oath, so Dando placed a black rock in his stomach."

"Kweli! Kweli!" shouted the crowd, their voices rising.

"So you see," concluded Asila, "you had better change your minds before the sun gets out of bed tomorrow. If you don't your lives won't be worth that–" He snapped his fingers to indicate how really useless they'd be.

Ndama was not afraid of the old man's magic. But he was afraid of being ambushed or poisoned. He knew that Dando would do anything–just anything to keep from losing face in front of his people.

2 Danger

A DIM LIGHT flickered through the twisted cracks in the door of their hut when Ochella and Ndama returned with Thuku. Afraid that Dando's men might be waiting inside to do them harm, Ndama carefully circled the hut listening for any suspicious sound. But the only sound he could hear was an occasional grunt of a hippo grazing nearby, and the loud report of a sleeping crocodile that let its jaws snap together. The report was louder than the one he had heard before, for it was early in the morning and most of the African wild was asleep.

Cautiously he slipped up to the door and knocked.

"Come in," answered a voice which he immediately recognized as Bwana Green's.

The boys entered with their guest to find their gray-haired missionary friend reading his worn Bible by the fire in the center of the floor. "Where have you been?" he asked, casting a suspicious glance at Thuku.

Ndama related the story, and then asked, "Why did it take you so long to return?"

"When I got to Kisumu," explained Green after he had thoughtfully pushed his fingers through his hair, "I called on Bwana D. C. (District Commissioner), and he told me of the trouble they've been having with the Luo and their old witch doctor, Dando. Then I was delayed a little more in getting some supplies for the mission at Bunyore."

He closed the Bible. "And so you've decided to be a follower of Jesu Christo," he said to Thuku, peering at him lovingly.

"Yes, Bwana Green," replied the man, biting his lip.

"But just saying that you are going to follow Him is not enough," said the missionary. "You must believe that He died for you, that He was raised from the dead for you. And you must give up heathenism, repent of your sins and change your ways. Have you done this?"

Thuku nodded. "Bwana Green, I know all these things. When I was no bigger than these boys I went to church at Ogada and the white missionary taught us much of the wisdom in the Book. My parents were believers and when they died the missionary preached their funerals. Ndama helped me see myself, and I now believe on Jesu Christo with all my heart. I'm truly sorry for the harm I've done in making others take the oath. I was afraid of the oath, but Ndama has helped me see that it has no power."

"If all of this is true we must pray together," said Green sinking to his knees.

All four of them prayed, and Ndama became convinced that Thuku had indeed repented of his sins and become a Christian.

"What I want to know," said Ochella, who had been silent up to this moment, "is what we are to do. These followers of Dando are very determined. They say they will drive the white man from Africa, and by the fierceness in their eyes I almost believe them."

"Bwana D. C. said that someone has told the Luo many lies about the white men," replied Green. "If we could find a way to talk to them and prove that the rumors are not true we could do something."

"But how will we get them to come together to listen?" asked Ndama, throwing up his hands in a gesture of despair. "They all believe Dando, and if he tells them not to come they won't come."

"Why don't you kill a hippo?" asked Thuku eagerly as he pointed to Green's gun leaning against the mud wall. "Last year a young man from Nairobi came and killed one. Then he pulled it up to the shore. You should have seen the people! They swarmed out like ants, and they took away the meat quicker than a woman can spit."

Green picked up his double-barreled rifle and thoughtfully examined it. "Do you think we'd have much trouble?"

"The lake's full of them," said Thuku. "If we'd get a boat we could shoot one without any trouble at all."

Green took the hard-nosed shells from the rifle chambers and placed them in the palm of his hand. He rolled them back and forth while he stared off into space. Then he slipped them back into the chamber and stood up. "I think that is a good plan," he said. "Just as soon as the sun is up, go out and get a boat–one big enough so that a hippo can't bite a hole in the bottom, and get a man to help you row it. We might have some trouble pulling the hippo in."

He then left the hut to go to the one where he usually spent the night.

As the boys curled up on the floor to sleep Thuku said, "Everything will be all right, I'm sure. The only thing that troubles my heart is that Dando threatened me. If I don't give up Jesu Christo by tomorrow night–"

"His medicine isn't any good," replied Ndama. "He couldn't hurt me, and he can't hurt you!"

"Do you really think this boat is big enough?" asked Green as he examined the large rowboat. "Hippo jaws are wide, and if one of them bit a hole in the bottom the crocodiles would eat us in no time."

"We got the biggest one we could find," replied Thuku, grinning until his big teeth glistened like polished cowrie shells. "My friend here, Ndombe, went with me and we looked at many boats.

Ndombe, a tall muscular man with unusually black skin, nodded his head vigorously. "This is the biggest one we could find," he said. "The lake is full of hippos, and we won't have to go out very far."

"Very well," said Green, "we'll go."

They took their places in the boat, and then Ndombe pushed them off from the sandy shore and leaped lightly into the boat. He picked up an oar and sat next to Thuku, and the two began to row.

The sun was just getting up in the east and as they moved out into the water they could see the distant buildings of Kisumu on the rim of the horizon. Most of the fishing boats had already gone in. But there were a few stragglers, and Ndama watched them as they moved toward the shore—their trim sails taut with the breeze.

Fishing was a thriving business at Kisumu, and many Arabs and Luo made their living this way. Some of the fish were sold fresh in the Kisumu and Luanda markets. Others were split in half, sun-dried, and peddled to distant villages by women who carried them on their heads in wide, traylike wicker baskets. Once, just after Bwana Green had driven by a number of women loaded with dry fish, he remarked to Ndama, "I don't see how people can eat them. They smell like an animal that has been dead a long time."

"How far will we have to go to find a hippo?" asked Ochella.

"We never know just where they are," said Thuku, "but we will find them very soon, I'm sure."

A snake swam by, its head just out of the water. Then Ndama noticed three or four crocodiles a few yards from the boat. Ndombe pointed to one with his oar. "*Piga* (shoot it), Bwana Green," he said.

"I don't want to waste my ammunition," replied the missionary shaking his head.

"Crocodiles are my special enemies," continued Ndombe. "I wish I could kill every one of the horrible brutes. Last week a friend of mine was out in the water fixing his nets when a crocodile grabbed him. We shouted at the top of our voices trying to make the monster let him go; but it was no use, we never saw my friend again.

"Less than a moon ago a white man from Eldoret shot one. I helped pull it in on the beach. He made us skin it, and when we cut the stomach open we found six wire bracelets. I'm sure that crocodile ate at least six people! Bwana Green, they are terrible. Their jaws are full of teeth, and their teeth are as sharp as razors. If one of them ever gets hold of you you'll never have to pay taxes anymore!"

Suddenly Ochella shouted, "There's a hippo!"

Instantly Bwana Green's rifle was at his shoulder and he was taking careful aim at the black skull of a hippo that was emerged a foot or so above the water less than fifty yards away. Then Ndama grabbed his shoulder and shouted, "Don't shoot! Don't shoot!"

"Why not?" demanded Green, aiming again.

Ndama pointed to a dozen black heads just in front of the boat. "Look at all those hippos," he cried, "If you'd wound one they'd attack and chew our boat into bits!"

The faces of Thuku and Ndombe showed that fear had clutched at their hearts. Ndama and Ochella closed their eyes and prayed.

"Let's get out of here!" commanded Green in a hoarse whisper.

Ndama watched the sweat pour from the faces of the men as they cautiously rowed away. When they were at a safe distance Bwana Green said, "It is good you saw those other hippos, Ndama. If you had not we'd now be dead."

They moved to another part of the lake, and here they hunted for several hours without seeing a single hippo.

There were many crocodiles, and Ndama watched them curiously as they swam by—their greedy eyes just above the water.

Ochella pointed to some approaching black clouds. "If we don't get out of here soon," he said, "we'll be caught in a storm."

"Be patient," replied Thuku, pointing to an island, "we'll get one pretty soon. They like to play around that island. I've been here before. I know."

Slowly they moved forward, the Luo dipping their oars into the water as silently as possible. Long-necked cranes flew overhead, and the tassel-topped papyrus on the island swayed in the breeze. There was a tiny splash on their right and Ndama noticed a large crocodile as it slithered from the dense undergrowth into the water.

All at once the men stopped rowing, and Ndombe pointed with his oar to a hippo's head a stone's throw away. Green raised his rifle to fire, but just as he was about to squeeze the trigger the head disappeared. In a moment it appeared at another spot. This time the whole head came out of the water and the big pachyderm yawned, opening its enormous mouth until its teeth were at least three feet apart. Bwana Green fired.

The head disappeared, and then the boat began to tremble. "What's causing that?" asked Ochella.

"The hippo is struggling with death," returned Thuku. "They do that every time unless the bullet kills them instantly."

As they sat in the boat waiting for the hippo to die, the sky became black with clouds, and a few drops of rain started to fall. "We'd better head for home," said Ochella nervously.

"But we can't go without the hippo!" exclaimed Ndama.

"How are we going to get it?" asked Green, facing the Luo.

"We'll just wait a bit," explained Thuku, "and it will

turn over on its back and come to the top. Then I'll tie a piece of wire into its jaw and we'll tow it."

By this time the falling rain had increased and the wind was blowing harder, sending waves that rocked the boat.

"We're in for a bad storm," said Ochella uneasily. "I sure wish we could get on our way. It'll take a long time to return—especially if we pull that hippo."

Thuku drew a dagger from its sheath and unwound a long piece of heavy wire. He tied the wire carefully into the thick metal ring attached to the stern just above the rudder. Then he prodded the water with his oar trying to locate the hippo. "It's coming up," he exclaimed suddenly. "I can feel it!"

They waited another few minutes and the hippo's feet began to emerge. Ndombe rowed closer to it so Thuku could reach into the water and pull the head to the surface. He cut a long slit in the lower jaw, threaded the wire through and wrapped it around itself several times so that it would not untwist and let go.

As he took his place at the oar a jagged streak of lightning burned across the sky and a second later there was a loud crash of thunder. "I sure hope we can make it back," said Ochella uneasily.

"We will, don't worry," assured Ndama confidently.

The hippo towed well, lying on its back—its short feet sticking in the air and wobbling slightly with the movement of the boat.

Thuku turned and glanced at it for a moment, and then he licked his lips. "That's one of the biggest ones I've ever seen," he said. "When you get that on the shore the people will come, and Dando won't be able to stop them. Hippo meat is really good!"

The rain began to fall in torrents and the boys had to start bailing. There was just enough rain to keep them busy. "We can keep the boat dry as long as the lake water stays out," said Ochella. "But what will we do if the wind increases and the waves start splashing in?"

"I'm an expert at running a boat," said Thuku. "I used to work for an Arab who was a fisherman. I've been in worse storms than this."

"But did you ever tow a hippo in a storm?" asked Ochella, as he emptied a can of water over the side.

If Thuku heard this question he didn't let on. He whispered to Ndombe, and the two of them began to row harder.

Several more flashes of lightning lit up the sky, and the thunder cracked like Bwana Green's gun. Then a stiff wind began to blow, rocking the boat back and forth. Waves came to within an inch of the top of the boat.

Ndama and Ochella worked harder, praying and bailing at the same time. But instead of letting up the rain increased. It poured from the sky like water from a pot.

Thuku and Ndombe began to sing. Their song was a wild one which Ndama had heard before on a native bus going from Luanda to Kisumu. The passengers had beat out the rhythm, pounding the palms of their hands on the metal sides of the vehicle. The words went:

Take me to Kisumu, Ungu Benjamin.

Take me for nothing, Ungu Benjamin.

The Ungu Benjamin, about whom they sang, was a Luo bus driver famous for his speed.

"They're singing to keep their hearts strong," said Ochella biting his lip.

Before Ndama could reply a big wave splashed into the boat, and the brothers had to work as hard as they could to bail it out. As they bailed the men sang louder than ever, and Ndama began to notice anxiety in their voices.

They had just thrown most of the water out when another wave came in and then another. They bailed furiously, working harder than they had ever worked before. But they could not throw it out as rapidly as it came in. Bwana Green searched for a can to help them, but there was none. Finally he took off his cork helmet and used that.

The water, however, was getting the best of them. Soon the boat would be so low the lake would pour in.

The shore was still a long way off, and as Ndama bailed he prayed that God would help them. But in spite of his prayer and faith he could not keep the thoughts of greedy crocodiles from entering his brain.

Thuku tried to steady the boat by pushing the rudder back and forth.

"That won't help!" warned Bwana Green, his voice rising with alarm. "Each time you move you rock the boat. You might break the rudder off!"

He had barely finished when another huge wave slopped over the side, drenching everyone.

"Bail faster!" shouted Ndama. "The water is rising right up to the edge of the boat!"

"I'm working as hard as I can!" replied Ochella.

Ndama dipped up the water and threw it out as fast as he could, but he didn't seem to be making any progress at all. Indeed, the water was right up to the seats and it seemed to be rising all the time. "If only we had bigger cans to dip with!" muttered Ndama, forcing himself to work even faster.

"But there aren't any other cans," replied Ochella. "We can't do the impossible!"

3 Strange Pulpit

I F YOU'LL UNTIE the hippo we can get the boat in," said Ndama frantically.

"But if we lose it there'll be no way to get the people out so that I can reason with them," replied Green, bailing as fast as he could.

"It would be better to get to shore without the hippo than to lose the hippo and be eaten too!" argued Ochella, his voice shaking.

The storm seemed to be letting up. Another wave splashed into the boat, but it wasn't as big as the others had been. "I think if we pray we can make it," shouted Green, speaking loudly in order to be heard above the din of the men who were singing about Ungu Benjamin at the tops of their voices. "But I'll cut the wire if you think we should."

"Let's wait for a few minutes," panted Ndama as he scooped the water out. "We're not too far from the shore and I believe we'll get there if we hold steady." He pointed with his can to a light that winked off and on.

"If another big wave comes we'll go under," protested Ochella.

"Well, I'm praying that another big wave won't come," replied Ndama grimly.

Thuku and Ndombe rowed as hard as they could,

and at the same time sang about the native bus driver. Another wave slopped into the boat, but it was a small one and they managed to bail the water out without the boat sinking.

As the light on the shore grew brighter their spirits rose.

"I wonder how far the light is?" asked Ochella.

"I don't know," muttered Ndama. "Lights always seem a lot closer than they are."

"Don't worry, boys," assured Green. "I'm sure the Lord has heard our prayer and He'll help us make the shore."

All at once the boat stopped moving, and the wire attached to the hippo became taut. "We've gotten to a shallow part," exclaimed Ndombe. "The hippo is dragging in the mud."

"What can we do?" asked Ndama.

"We'll just have to pull it through," said Thuku.

The Luo bent their backs at the oars and gradually the boat moved forward. Then there was a slight jerk as the hippo slid off the obstruction.

"Thank God, we got over that," murmured Ndama.

"I wonder where the crocodiles go in a storm like this," said Ochella.

"I wish I knew," said Green.

The hippo got stuck again, and again they had a hard time in working it loose. But the storm was definitely over, and they were close enough to the shore to see shadowy figures moving in front of the fires that burned at the waterfront.

They didn't get stuck again until they were within speaking distance of the shore. This time Thuku shouted to the waiting Luo, asking them to get a rope and help pull them in.

Soon two young men came wading through the water with a big coil of sisal rope. "Aren't they afraid of crocodiles?" asked Ochella.

"Of course they're afraid," laughed Ndombe, "but they know we have enough meat to fill their stomachs for two or three days and they're glad to take the risk!"

Thuku untied the wire from the metal ring and tied it to the rope. Then he signaled for the men to pull the hippo in. While they were doing this, he and Ndombe pushed the boat up onto the beach. There were at least one hundred men waiting, each one armed with a heavy dagger.

The moment the hippo was out of the water they were on top of it, slashing at the meat with their knives.

"Tell the people to wait, that I want to talk to them before they get the meat," said Green to Ndama.

Ndama interpreted what Green had said, but it had no effect on the crowd. They went after the hippo like vultures, each one determined to get more than the other. One man cut off a big slab of flesh and handed it to a woman. Then he cut off another and handed it to another woman. He then went after the head, but the moment he got his knife into the neck someone else had the same idea. Soon, instead of slashing at the hippo they were fighting with one another. At that moment a native came out of the bush onto the shore wearing a red fez. Those who saw him bowed in respect.

He strode over to the fighting men, and calmly boxed their ears. The men thus treated stepped back and eyed each other angrily. Then the stranger walked up to Green and in perfect Swahili said, "I am Chief Mugo, the chief of this country, and I'm sorry for the way these people act. One man, whose ears I just boxed, has three wives. He has been using them to get all the meat. I am ashamed that he is so selfish. We are thankful that you used your thunderstick to kill the meat, and if there is anything we can do for you we'll be glad to do it."

"Thank you very much, Chief Mugo," replied Bwana Green. "One of the reasons I killed the hippo was that I wanted to talk to the people. I wish you'd ask them to stand still while I speak. Tell them when I'm through they can have all the meat, that I don't want any myself."

Mugo climbed on top of the hippo, and standing on the ribs with as much dignity as he could manage under the circumstances, translated what Bwana Green had said.

There was a soft murmur of grumbling, but there were also many who nodded their heads respectfully; and Ndama was sure most of them would obey their chief.

After the crowd had quieted the missionary motioned for Ndama to interpret, and then he took his place on top of the partly butchered hippo. "We are here to speak to you and to tell you we are your friends," he began. "I know there are white people who have not done right to the Africans. But because one white man is bad they are not all bad. There are some of your people who are better than others. I am your friend."

"I don't believe it!" shouted Asila angrily as he elbowed his way through the crowd to the front. "All the white people are the same. The only thing they think about is making us pay taxes. I never saw a good crocodile, and I never saw a good white man!"

He would have continued in this fashion, but Mugo went over and silenced him.

"I have lived at Bunyore many years," continued Green calmly. "If you visit the mission and ask the people they will tell you I have done all I can to help them. We have a hospital for those who are sick. We feed the patients and do all we can to make them well, and we never charge them."

"Dando has better medicines than you!" shouted Asila.

Mugo shook his shoulder angrily and demanded that he keep still. But Asila ignored him and kept talking. Finally the chief borrowed a thick knobkerrie from a friend and threatened Asila with it. Asila's face darkened, and his eyes blazed with a horrible fury—reminding Ndama of the lion that had seized him at Chiberaria. He started to say something. Then he thought better of it and left. When he got to the edge of the crowd he pointed at Green and pulled his finger across his throat as if he were slitting it.

"If you will let us speak to you as friends," said Green after Asila had disappeared, "we will teach you many things about God and how He sent His only Son, Jesu Christo, to die for men and women and boys and girls.

"We are going to return to our huts, and tomorrow, after the sun gets out of bed, if any of you want to come and visit us we'll be very happy for you to come."

As he stepped down from this strange pulpit many of the people nodded, indicating that they would come. But in an instant Dando was on top of the hippo. "Anyone who goes and talks to this white man," he said, "will be in danger of his life! My medicines are very strong, much stronger than the white man's. I'm making a terrible medicine right now. It is so strong I can kill anyone with it even though they are a long way off. These words are meant for everyone—even Chief Mugo!"

After this last statement he slowly turned his head, studying everyone in the crowd. He rattled the magic charms he wore around his neck, then disappeared into the darkness.

"Do you think anyone will come tomorrow?" asked Green, as he sat cross-legged by the fire in the hut where the boys stayed.

"One or two *might* come," ventured Thuku, "but I doubt very much if others will come. Dando is too powerful."

"Even if they don't come," put in Ndama, "I think we did a lot of good, and I have a feeling that Mugo is on our side."

"Mugo might be on your side *now*," returned Thuku, "but when Dando starts threatening him with his magic he'll change. Mugo is a good man, but he's afraid of

Dando. He usually gets his advice before he makes any decisions."

"Do you remember how he said that if you didn't give up the new religion by tonight he'd do something to you?"

"I remember," replied Thuku nervously. "I'm just hoping that he'll forget about it."

"I wouldn't be worried about his medicines," said Green. "Without a doubt he could kill you by putting poison in your food, but his other type of medicine has no power—"

"Bwana Green, his medicines are very powerful," interrupted Thuku. "Last year he got angry at a man because he went to another witch doctor, and by merely saying some magic words and hanging a frog in front of the man's door he killed him. He is more to be feared than a crocodile!"

"He didn't kill us," said Ndama.

"That's true, but your medicine is stronger than his," argued Thuku, casting a sidelong glance at Green.

Bwana Green pulled out the Gospel of John. "This book has the most power of all," he said. "You have accepted Jesu Christo, and He has promised to look after us. He knows when a sparrow falls, and He loves you a lot more than a little bird."

"I know that's true—but I still have some doubts," returned Thuku slowly. "Remember my father was afraid of the witch doctor and so was my grandfather. They taught me these things from the time I was a little child. It's hard to give them up, but I'll try—"

"The best thing we can do about it is to pray," said the missionary getting on his knees.

All four of them prayed, each one mentioning Thuku's problem. Thuku, himself, prayed earnestly, and Ndama felt assured he'd be protected.

When they got to their feet Green said, "If the Lord doesn't answer prayer we're all sunk. Bwana D. C. told me that if the natives attacked us he wouldn't send any soldiers; that the government wouldn't be held responsible for our safety."

"Then we'd better *really* pray!" said Ochella warmly.

Green smiled at them. "We'll be all right," he affirmed confidently. "I'm now going to the other hut to get some sleep. Don't worry about the secret society or about the Luo. God will take care of us!"

The sun was a fourth of the way up in the sky when Ndama opened his eyes. He got up and opened the door so the light would come in. Then he looked at the spot where Thuku had slept, and gave a low whistle. The tall Luo who had just professed to be a Christian was gone!

Quickly he stepped outside, looking for his friend. Then he whistled again, for, dangling from the grass roof by a thin piece of banana bark was a dead frog! A gentle breeze was moving it back and forth in front of the door.

"Ochella," shouted Ndama, "come and look at this!"

"Wh-what do y-you th-think it means?" asked his younger brother, shocked wide awake by the sight.

"I only wish I knew," replied Ndama thoughtfully. "Let's go and tell Bwana Green!"

They slipped quietly into his hut and found that he was still on the floor sleeping, an army blanket pulled up to his chin. They were in the act of leaving when Ochella suddenly gasped, "Look, Ndama," he whispered, "his gun is gone!"

The blood drained from Ndama's face as he cast his eyes around the tiny room searching for the missing weapon. "He usually stands it by his head," he said at last.

"Wh-what do you want?" asked Green, opening his eyes and stretching himself awake.

"We wanted to tell you that Thuku is gone and your gun is missing," said Ochella all in one gulp.

Green glanced at the spot where the gun had been. "I wonder what could have happened to it," he said. He looked around the room and scratched his head. Then he went to his khaki jacket. "Let's see if the thief got any ammunition," he muttered while he thrust his hands into the side pockets. "Well, I guess he did," he added weakly. "Now we're really in a jam!"

"Do you th-think Thuku was just a spy?" asked Ndama.

"I'm sure I don't know," returned the missionary.

"Last night when you mentioned that the government wouldn't send any soldiers to help us if we got into trouble I noticed a funny look come into Thuku's face," said Ndama. "If he spreads that kind of information around, the people will think they can do anything to us and get away with it!"

Bwana Green dressed, put on his water-soaked helmet and stepped out of the hut. Ndama pointed to the dead frog. "It may be that Thuku is our friend after all. Perhaps someone put that frog there to kill him, and when he saw it he was so scared he ran for his life."

The missionary jerked it loose and threw it into the bush. "I don't know what to think," he said. "But I do know we're in God's will and He will take care of us!"

A twig broke behind them. Ndama whirled to see what it was. And at that moment Chief Mugo stepped out of the brush and approached them. He was dressed just as he had been with the exception that his head was bare.

"I have come to talk to you," he said, holding out his hand to the missionary.

With the sunlight playing on his face Ndama noticed something he had not been able to see the night before because of the darkness. His large brown eyes were filled with infection, and when he spoke to the missionary he squinted, indicating that he couldn't see very well.

"Do you think you could help my eyes?" he asked hopefully.

Green stepped a little closer and pulled his eyes open with his fingers while he studied the problem. "I think I can help you," he said quietly. "Ndama, you go into my hut and bring the medicine chest."

Ndama placed the wooden box in front of the missionary and unlocked the lid. Green then made up a solution and put several drops in the chief's eyes. "This medicine won't cure you all at once," he said when he was through. "You'll have to come back every day for at least a week, and even then you might not be cured but I think this will help."

"Thank you very much, Bwana White Man," said Mugo, bowing low in front of the missionary. "I will come back every day just as you say, and I hope Dando doesn't cause you too much trouble." He stroked his chin thoughtfully. Then he added, "If the medicine you have in the square box and in the bundle of white leaves is stronger than his you have nothing to worry about. But Dando is a very powerful man. Be careful!"

The native ruler slipped back into the bushes, and was soon lost from sight.

Soon the conversation returned to Thuku and the impending danger. Then a low whistle attracted Ndama's attention. It sounded like a quail, but was not quite real. Suspiciously he stepped to the edge of the clearing. And then he saw a Luo boy about his own age. The boy advanced slowly toward him, looking this way and that as if he were afraid he was being followed. And then he handed Ndama a stick and immediately vanished into the undergrowth.

The stick had been split on the end, and a letter inserted. Ndama was used to this kind of "envelope." He had used them to carry mail himself. Holding the letter in the end of the stick kept it from getting soiled from sweaty fingers. But he was curious to know who would be writing him there, and why the carrier was so anxious to get away. Generally the one who delivered the letter waited for baksheesh. Anyone who didn't, Ndama thought, must have a very strong reason!

H IS PULSE racing, Ndama motioned for Ochella and Green to follow and led the way into the missionary's hut. He ripped the letter from the stick and held it up to the light coming in the open door.

His first thought was that it was a letter from Bunyore, telling him that his father was sick and that he should hurry back. Then he noted Thuku's name at the bottom!

"Hurry up and read it!" said Ochella anxiously.

Ndama held the letter a little closer and read:

Dear Friends:

Come and help me at once, and bring the Book with the story of Jesu Christo. The boy who brought the letter will show you the way. I've told him to wait for you by the baobab tree. Don't delay. I'm in very great danger!

Thuku

"What do you think it means?" asked Ndama, as he scanned the letter again.

"I think it's a trick!" exclaimed Ochella. "Thuku is just a spy. He wants one of us to go out so he can use him as a hostage!"

"That may be true," put in Green slowly, "but again it may not be. I do think the one who goes with the boy will be risking his life, but I think it's a chance we must take. Will either of you volunteer?"

There was a deep silence in the hut as the boys thought this over. Both of them knew the secret society was desperate, and both of them knew the Luo could easily throw them to the crocodiles and then say the monsters had grabbed them on their own.

At last Ndama said, "I'll go. God has protected me before, and He'll protect me now.

"But I still can't understand why I'm to meet this guide under the baobab tree. It would have been just as easy to have met him right here."

"It would be easier to kidnap you that far from us," said Ochella. "I wonder what kind of danger it is that he faces. Is it the danger of the oath? You know they vowed that if they didn't do what Dando told them to do, the oath would kill them. Or is he afraid of Dando's threat about giving up Jesu Christo?"

"I don't know now," said Ndama grimly. "But I'll know pretty soon." He got to his feet to leave.

"Let's have prayer first," said the missionary motioning them back. The trio knelt by the fire after Bwana Green had closed the door and each one of them prayed. When they got up from their knees the missionary laid an affectionate hand on Ndama's shoulder. "Do you still think you should go?" he asked.

"I'm more certain than ever," he replied.

"Then, we'll continue to pray for you," said Green. "If you are certain you are in God's will everything will be all right."

Ndama waited at the baobab tree for several minutes before the guide showed up. "My name is Pipa," he said, smiling and holding out his hand. The thin-faced boy seemed to appear from nowhere.

Ndama introduced himself, and then he said, "Let's go." He watched Pipa carefully, trying to find a clue to his intentions. But if he had any ideas at all Ndama couldn't make them out. He led the way through the tall grass on his spindly legs as if he had a job to do, but had no idea of the reason.

"How far is it?" ventured Ndama cautiously.

"It's a long way," returned Pipa, his voice as emotionless as the grunt of a hippo.

"Is Thuku well?"

"I don't know. You'll find out when you get there."

He wanted to ask him about the gun, but after further thought decided such a question would not be wise. They had been walking for about an hour when they came to a small hill with a large, well-kept village on top.

"The big hut in the center on the very top is Chief Mugo's," said Pipa, after he'd led Ndama on a small path that forked off the main one. "His hut is the biggest one around. He's very proud of it. I've never been inside, but I hope to be some day."

Encouraged by this much conversation, Ndama asked, "How does Mugo get along with Dando?"

"I don't know," returned Pipa, scowling darkly.

They continued on, passing through an area of dense underbrush, a small fertile valley and over three or four rolling hills. Finally they came to a small cave that opened in the red-brick side of a gulch. The opening was just large enough for a man to wriggle through and was partially hidden from view by heavy scrub. Pipa pointed inside. "Your friend, Thuku, is in there," he said.

Ndama started to thank the guide, but before he could utter a word he had disappeared as mysteriously as he had come.

"You'd better come in before you're seen," said Thuku from the inside.

Ndama gulped at the thought of crawling into such

a place, knowing that he would be at the complete mercy of the one inside. But there was nothing else to do!

The cave was much larger on the inside than he had imagined. There was not enough room to stand up, but there was plenty of space for a dozen people provided they remained in a sitting position.

"How did you get here?" asked Ndama, after his eyes had become accustomed to the darkness.

"I had just gotten up and gone outside when a man seized me," explained Thuku, speaking very excitedly.

"When I asked him what he wanted he said that Dando had sent him to tie a frog on our hut. And I think you know what a frog will do. It is one of the most terrible of all curses!"

"But how did you get here?"

"I wrestled with him until I broke away, and then I ran. I was in such a hurry I almost bumped into a grazing hippo, but the Lord helped me and here I am." His voice went higher and higher as he spoke, and his eyes widened until the whites seemed to fill his face.

"Did you take Bwana Green's gun?"

"What did you say?" demanded Thuku, grabbing Ndama's shoulder.

Ndama repeated the question.

"N-no I-I didn't," he declared, as if such a thing was impossible. "I didn't even know it was gone–"

"Who was the boy who brought me here?"

"Oh, he's a cousin of mine."

"Aren't you afraid he'll tell Dando where you are?"

"He wouldn't do that. Anyway, Dando doesn't care. He knows his medicine can kill me wherever I am. That's why I called you."

"He can't kill you with medicine unless he puts it in your food," replied Ndama.

"But he used the frog, and I've disobeyed the oath!"

"Don't be afraid of the oath, it has no power!"

"Does the B-book s-say that?" he asked eagerly.

"It most certainly does! Here, I'll read it to you," said Ndama after he'd opened the New Testament to I John. He pointed to the seventh verse of the first chapter and read the last portion of the verse, "...and the blood of Jesus Christ cleanseth us from all sin."

"Read it again," said Thuku, his eyes staring into space. Ndama read it again and emphasized the word, *all.*

Thuku jerked the book away from him and read the portion himself. Then he exclaimed, "Does it really mean that?"

"It most certainly does!" returned Ndama warmly.

"But the oath. Does it include the oath?" asked Thuku, a shadow of doubt spreading over his face.

"That text means that *all* sin is cleansed," said Ndama. "All means everything. It includes *all* sin. It means the oath was forgiven when you confessed your sins to Jesu Christo. It has no more power over you. You don't have to obey it or be afraid of it!"

"This is wonderful!" shouted Thuku so loudly Ndama had to caution him to lower his voice. "This means the oath I made cannot touch me. What a relief this is. I feel as light as a scrap of paper."

"About the gun," said Ndama. "Where do you think it is?"

"Maybe the man who brought the frog took it–" returned Thuku. He started to say something else. His lips formed a word but no sound came. After what seemed a full minute he took Ndama's hands and pointing to the New Testament said, "Is there any place in the Book where it says God will protect us from the witch doctor's magic?"

Ndama felt cold sweat on the man's hands, and he knew his answer would be very important. He prayed that God would help him find a suitable scripture. Then he slowly opened the New Testament to Colossians and read the thirteenth verse of the first chapter, "Who hath delivered us from the *power of darkness,* and hath translated us into the kingdom of his dear Son."

Thuku demanded that he read it again. Then he read it himself. Soon the fear vanished from his face. "I'm not afraid of Dando's silly frogs anymore," he said, hitting the palm of his hand with his doubled fist.

"Now I want to know about the gun," said Ndama returning to the subject. "Do any of your people know how to shoot one?"

Thuku scratched his head thoughtfully. "The only one I can think of who might is Ndege. He used to be a policeman in Kisumu. Bwana D. C. sent him home after he had been in jail for stealing."

"Whoever took the gun must have known how to shoot it, because they took ammunition too," said Ndama. "Do you think Ndege could have been the one who brought the frog and grabbed you?"

"I-I really don't know. It was too dark to see him well. B-but it could have been."

"Do you know of anyone else who would know about guns?"

"N-no he's the only one."

"Then we're going over to his hut and get it back!"

"Ndama!" exclaimed Thuku. "You are my friend. Don't even think such a thought. I was present when Ndege took the oath. His hatred is deep—very deep!"

"There is no other way," said Ndama, preparing to leave the cave. "If he leads the people with the gun there will be many who will be murdered, and Bwana Green will be in trouble with the government for losing the gun. Come! God will take care of us. Do you know where Ndege lives?"

"Y-yes I kn-know where he lives, but if we go there it will be—be like walking into a crocodile's jaws!"

Instead of answering Ndama crawled out of the cave. "Lead the way," he commanded.

"All right," returned Thuku hoarsely, "but let's crawl so we won't be seen."

As they crawled along Ndama kept praying that God would help them reach Ndege's hut and recover the gun without being seen. Suddenly they saw a woman approaching with a large black pot of milk on her head.

Ndama grabbed Thuku by the heel. "We'd better stand," he whispered, "or she'll be suspicious."

They got to their feet just as the woman rounded the corner by a huge anthill that was eight or ten feet high.

"Musawa," she greeted in Jaluo.

Ndama and Thuku returned the greeting. She stepped aside for them to pass, and as she did so she slopped some of the milk out of the pot down onto her neck.

When they were out of sight again they got on their knees and continued to crawl. Ndama prayed that she wouldn't think anything was out of the way and report them.

They had been moving along in this fashion for perhaps an hour when the sound of drums came to their ears. Thuku listened carefully. Then he said, "It sounds like the drums are in Ndege's village. They are calling people to a meeting. Ndama, we'd better not go on!"

"Don't be afraid, Thuku. We'll be all right," chided Ndama. "I'm not afraid. The most they can do is to kill our bodies, and then our souls will go to be with the Lord forever!"

The sound of drums got louder as they inched forward. Twice they had to get to their feet because of approaching women. And once they had to disappear into the grass when some armed warriors trotted by, moving in the direction of the drums.

Ndama knew he hadn't eaten for a long time, but he had no feeling of hunger. He could think of only two things: to recover the gun and to discover Dando's plans. He realized the danger he was facing, but he had great faith that with God's help he would be successful.

Soon they were on top of a little hill, and from this

vantage point they could see Ndege's village below and the great lake beyond. There was a large circle of men at the side of the main house, and it seemed someone was speaking to them.

"Let's get closer so we can hear what they have to say," said Ndama.

Thuku clutched Ndama's wrist. "Don't you have any fear?" he demanded. His voice was ragged with impatience.

"I've faced worse danger than this," said Ndama boastfully. "I was once even carried in a lion's jaws. Come on! Let's get closer."

A thick belt of heavy grass skirted the village. Ndama decided their best way was to hide in the grass, hear what the men had to say; then, when there was opportunity, slip into Ndege's hut and search for the rifle. When he mentioned this plan to Thuku, the Luo's face became troubled with fear and the whites of his eyes showed wider than ever. He tried to argue, but Ndama had made up his mind.

Cautiously they worked themselves down the hill and into the grass. Each time they stopped Thuku insisted they had gone far enough—that further advances meant instant death. But Ndama would not give up. "I'm going to get so close there will be only ten blades of grass between us!" he whispered.

The sound of voices was now very clear. But Ndama wanted to see those who spoke. He wriggled forward and peered through the grass into the open spaces around the huts. It seemed that there were at least fifty men present—most of them warriors. Dando, dressed in all his finery, was standing near a grain storage hut addressing them.

"We must do all we can to get rid of the white man," he said. "They have ruined our country and stolen our land, and are teaching our young people new ways. They tell everyone their medicine is better than ours. And they are so cunning in what they say many of our sick people are going to them instead of coming to us."

"We should also get hold of Thuku. He should be fed to the crocodiles for he is a traitor and has accepted the new religion."

Ndama glanced across to see how Thuku was taking this. Thuku's eyes widened and sweat was pouring from his shoulders and streaming down his back. Feeling the terror that gripped his friend, Ndama prayed that God would give the man courage.

"I also wish someone would get these boys who work for the white man," continued Dando. "They are troublemakers. Both of them should be thrown to the crocodiles, especially Ndama. And I want all of you to promise that you won't eat or drink or sleep until all three of them are out of the way.

"Will you make that promise?"

"*Kweli! Kweli!* We make the promise," they all answered together.

"Are any of these people members of the secret society?" whispered Ndama.

"Almost all of them are members," replied Thuku hoarsely. "Ndama, let's get away while we have a chance!"

"We are Christians and we won't run," replied Ndama, holding Thuku by the leg.

"But I know a lot of those people," pled Thuku. "They are very determined, and they would as soon throw us to the crocodiles as to spit. They–"

"Which one of the huts is Ndege's?" asked Ndama, ignoring Thuku's demand.

"The center one–the one with the door facing away from the crowd. But don't try to go in! You'll be seen, and then they'll get both of us!"

"Oh, no they won't," replied Ndama.

"Yes, they will, Ndama," pled Thuku.

"Listen!" said Ndama firmly. "I am going to crawl into that hut and get that gun, and I don't want you to try and stop me. If you do, we'll be discovered!"

"The only thing I want you to do is be quiet, and to pray!"

5 Flight

HE MOVED THE grass apart just enough to make a better survey. The warriors' spears were stuck in the ground on the same side of the village where the men were seated. This meant that if he were discovered the men would have to go for their spears before they could start the chase. Ndama knew this was not much advantage, but it was some. The tall grass extended far enough so that he would be covered most of the time. The only time he would be exposed would be when he would step from the clearing to the side of the hut. Once he had gotten this far he could slip around the side and into the door without being seen. Of course there was a chance that someone might be in the hut, but he would have to risk it!

He decided the safest way was to crawl from the grass to the hut. He knew there would be a proper time to do this. He prayed that God would give him wisdom to know just the right time.

The men were chattering with one another on numerous subjects: the secret society, the price of fish and the rain. As they spoke they looked in various directions. Ndama knew that if he stepped out then he would most certainly be seen. He prayed again for help. Then Asila got up and walked over to the place where the speakers had stood. Soon every eye was on him.

"It is more important to get rid of Ndama and Ochella than it is for it to rain," he said. His snarling words were full of hate. "These boys are the worst kind of boys, for they work for the white man and believe in his foolish talk about Jesu Christo."

Ndama knew that this was his opportunity. Quickly he crawled out of the grass into the open and headed toward the hut, his eyes on the speaker. He wanted to make as little noise as possible, but because he was watching the speaker, he accidentally knelt on a dry stick. It snapped, making a noise like that of a crocodile's jaws. The speaker paused as if he had heard a sound, and Ndama felt the hairs on the back of his neck curl forward.

He lay on his stomach, afraid to move. His heart beat so loud he was afraid it would be heard. Then the speaker continued with his discourse. "Remember, we promised not to eat or drink or sleep until these boys are inside the crocodiles. If anyone does, Dando will put a curse on them!"

But Ndama wasn't listening. He was thinking only of getting the gun back to Bwana Green. In a moment he was at the side of the hut, and hidden from view. Slowly he inched forward, pausing every time the speaker paused.

He worked himself around the hut, and slipped inside. At first he could see nothing because of the smoke and darkness, and as he waited for his eyes to become accustomed to the darkness he had a gnawing in the pit of his stomach because of fear that someone was in the hut watching him. Gradually he began to see, and then he breathed a sigh of relief for the hut was empty. His problem now was to find the gun and get back into the grass without being seen!

The acrid smoke of a smoldering fire in the center of the floor bit into his eyes and nostrils. There were several big water pots on his right. He peered behind them, but the gun wasn't there. Then he lifted the blanket on the cow dung-covered floor and there it was, and the box of ammunition was right beside it! With a cry of joy he cradled the rifle in his arms and slipped the heavy ammunition in his back pocket.

He started for the door, and then there was a terrible clatter. The stock of the gun had bumped into an aluminum kettle on the wall and it fell to the ground! Instantly the hum of voices from the outside stopped and a voice shouted, "What was that?" Another voice cried, "I don't know, but I'll soon find out!"

Desperately Ndama looked for a place to hide. But there was none. The only possible protection was the six-inch-thick pole that supported the cone-shaped roof from the middle of the floor. A man would have to have bad eyes not to see him behind that, unless, of course, he didn't stay long enough for his eyes to adjust to the darkness. He thought of defending himself with the rifle. He had never fired it, but he knew how to slip a cartridge into the chamber and pull the trigger. But he knew that Bwana Green would never allow it to be pointed at anyone.

Quickly he jumped behind the pole, standing sideways to the door in order to have the greatest possible safety. He knew that this was like a leopard hiding behind a piece of straw, but it was the best he could do! The sound of steps grew louder, and then a man bent over and looked inside.

Ndama held his breath, wondering what he would do.

"I think one of your pans fell from the wall," he said over his shoulder to the crowd of men behind.

"Maybe I'd better go inside," said a voice which Ndama recognized as Asila's. "There is no need to take chances. These boys who work for Bwana White Man are pretty clever."

As the man crawled inside Ndama prayed that God

would help him to escape. He knew that one little sound, a cough or a loud breath would give him away. He stood as rigidly as possible, his eyes slanted sideways watching the approaching member of the secret society.

Asila straightened up just inside the door, and quickly surveyed the hut. He started to leave, and then thought better of it. He stepped to within inches of the pole and swept his eyes around—peering into every corner. Ndama could feel and smell Asila's alcoholic breath.

Right then he knew he could see Asila, but that Asila probably could not see him. In two or three seconds, however, the Luo's eyes would dilate, and he would be seen. He prayed that he would leave before this happened. And then another fear gripped him. He couldn't hold his breath much longer. Soon he would have to take a deep breath or black out!

Asila looked around again, and then he struck the pole with his fist and left. He muttered something at the door but Ndama didn't quite catch it.

Soon another speaker was lecturing the men, and Ndama filled his lungs with air. Now, he simply had to crawl out of the hut, slip over the open space and vanish into the grass. He waited until he felt that everyone's eyes would be on the one making the speech, and then with a prayer in his heart, crawled out of the door. He crept around the side of the hut, pausing every foot or two to make sure the way was clear. When he got to the place where he would be exposed to view the speaker thundered, "If I have to lose all my possessions in order to get rid of the white man I will lose them. I will even be glad to part with my life. Let all who will agree to do this with me say *mmmm*."

The crowd uttered a loud *mmmm*, and at that moment Ndama made a dash for the grass. Ordinarily he would have made this distance without any trouble, but this time he tripped over a stick and fell sprawling on the ground. In an instant a man shouted, "There's one of the white man's boys and he has the gun. Get him!"

As Ndama got to his feet he could see the warriors dashing for their spears. He gripped the rifle as firmly as possible and ran for his life–heading first for the grass.

He had seen a band of men chase a mongoose and had wondered how the mongoose felt. Now he knew. He had the advantage of perhaps one hundred and fifty feet, but he was tired and many of the warriors were grown men and used to the chase. A snake slithered by as he leaped into the grass. He knew that his only possible means of escape was his cunning, but at this moment he could think of nothing. The grass was high enough for him to hide in. But if he did this the Luo would simply cut it down and he would be trapped as he had frequently seen a leopard trapped.

"Go to the other side, and get him when he comes through," shouted Asila confidently.

Ndama saw three warriors obey this command. As they ran to the other side to cut off his retreat he could see the white metal heads of their spears flashing in the fierce sunlight. It was hard to wade through the tall grass– his bare feet were filled with thorns–but he knew it was his only chance. He stumbled on, falling and rising– heading for the opposite side of the belt. "Get him! Get him!" shouted the men, a shrill note of triumph in their voices. Ndama prayed for strength and wisdom, and then he glanced over his shoulder and found the men were slowly gaining on him. He tried to make his feet move faster, but he simply could not. He could now see the path that he intended to follow. This increased his strength some and he made a mighty lunge forward. But those who had gone to cut him off were nearing the place where he would reach the path.

"Oh, God, help me!" he prayed.

The moment he touched the path the three Luo were less than thirty feet away. He knew he could whirl around and face them with the rifle. They had seen the way it had spoken death to the hippo and he knew they had respect for it. But Bwana Green had preached that this was not his way—that it was better to die than to use a gun against human beings.

There was no grass to hinder him on the path, but the thorns in his feet stabbed with pain every time he put them down.

The whole crowd was now behind him, shouting and yelling like savage fiends. Ndama felt a pain in his side, but he gritted his teeth and prayed for strength to run faster. The strength, however, did not come.

Despair and fear flowed through his veins, and he felt he must give up. Then he noticed a heavy branch right across the path a few feet ahead. How it had gotten there he did not know, but it blocked his way. He knew now how an animal feels when it's trapped and the screaming hunters are right behind.

"We've got him! We've got him!" shouted the man nearest him.

But at that moment Ndama got an idea. He leaped over the end of the branch, and then quickly pushed the end farther into the grass so as to put the biggest part in front of the warriors. This clever maneuver helped him gain fifty or sixty feet—and with this advantage he got new strength.

On and on he went, gaining slowly all the time. Then a small hill loomed up in front. The top of the hill would hide him from his pursuers. He decided that if the path leading down the hill was straight he'd have to keep going, but if it curved so that anyone going around the curve could not be seen from the top of the hill he would leap into the grass and hide. The men then, he hoped, would keep on going; and he could slip back on the path he had followed toward Ndege's village.

In almost no time he was at the top of the incline where he would have to make his decision—a decision that would mean life or death. He took in the situation at a glance. The path did curve a few feet ahead by a tall anthill, and the grass that lined the path in this area was tall enough to hide a boy his size from view.

Without hesitation he flung himself into the tall grass and pressed his body to the earth as low as possible. But even then, he knew that anyone who looked closely could see the flattened grass and discover him.

The patter of feet grew louder, and then they rushed by. Ndama then leaped from his hiding place, and in a crouched position fled in the opposite direction as fast as possible. The prayer of thanks he prayed again and again kept time with his racing feet.

He continued on in this direction until he thought it was safe to follow another that led to Bwana Green's hut.

The missionary listened to this story with amazement. Then he said, "Chief Mugo has been getting much better, and he is on our side. The witch doctor has been working against him for years, and he told me that if he does anything to us he shouldn't do he'll send word to Bwana D. C. in Kisumu. He said that Dando knows this, and will be careful. And so, I think, it will be safe for you to stay here…"

A knock at the door interrupted their conversation. Ndama opened it just wide enough to see. Then he exclaimed, "Come in, Thuku!"

As Thuku entered he felt Ndama's hands and feet as if he thought he was a ghost. Finally he became composed enough to ask, "How did you get away?"

Ndama explained his escape, mentioning only the main points.

"Did you get the gun and the bullets?"

Ndama pointed to the rifle by the missionary's medicine chest, and then he touched his back pocket which bulged with ammunition.

Thuku shook his head with wonder. "Surely God was with you," he said.

"I think we should pray and give God thanks," suggested Green.

Everyone agreed to this, and each one, including Ochella who had been silent up to this point, thanked the heavenly Father for His care.

When they got up from their knees Thuku said, "Chief Mugo will give you some protection here, but I don't think he'll help me. I had bad words with him a few moons ago, and I think he'd be happy for me to be caught by Dando and his men."

"What do you think we should do?" asked Ochella.

"I think the best plan would be to take me to Kisumu in a boat," he said. "I have a friend there who will care for me until this trouble has blown away."

"When do you want to go?" asked Ndama.

"I think I should go tonight!"

"But how will we find the way?"

"We can row toward the Kisumu lights."

"Yes, but how will I get back?"

"You can stay with my friend and return in the morning. You'd know the way back in daylight, wouldn't you?"

"I-I think s-so," returned Ndama nervously.

"But where is the boat?" asked Ochella.

"Don't worry about that," said Thuku, "I'll have one ready—a small one with two oars. I know just where it is."

Bwana looked at the watch on his wrist. "It is now five o'clock," he said. "If Ndama is to take you, you'd both better get some rest and some food to eat. Ochella, make a pot of *obusuma* (mush)."

The sun was a dull glowing ball in the west, its lower half below the horizon, when the missionary shook Ndama and Thuku awake.

"If you're going to leave you'd better leave now," he said. "If you wait any longer you'll be too late to get into the home of your friend in Kisumu." He pointed to the heaping plate of *obusuma* Ochella had prepared.

Ndama and Thuku ate like starved dogs, and Ochella teased them about their appetites.

"We're not eating so much because the food is cooked well," countered Ndama. "We're just hungry!"

They finished their meal, and then cautiously slipped out into the blackness toward the boat Thuku had ready. Walking without a light in an area where hippos and crocodiles moved about was dangerous business, but Ndama was used to dangerous business!

6 Crocodile Jaws

$\mathbf{B}$E CAREFUL where you step," warned Thuku, "many crocodiles like to sleep around here." He led the way down to a sandy part of the beach and there, beneath a large palm tree, he pointed to the boat.

Ndama got in and picked up an oar. "I hope we don't have any storms," he said.

"Don't worry, we'll be all right," assured Thuku. "It won't take us long to get there."

The two of them bent their backs to the oars and headed toward the dancing lights in the distance. "Did you ever make this trip before?" ventured Ndama uneasily.

"Many times," replied Thuku.

"Who is this friend, and what does he do?" asked Ndama, pausing with a dripping oar in his hand.

"His name is Okweli, and he drives a truck for an Indian."

They continued to row for an hour or more before Ndama felt the boat touch sand on the Kisumu side. Here, Thuku tied the boat to a handful of grass and led the way up the path that connected to one of Kisumu's main streets. Thuku knew the city well, and as they walked along the asphalt pavement he knew just where to turn.

Okweli was glad to see them, and with enthusiasm threw open the door of his corrugated-iron shanty. He insisted that they eat and brought out a plate of roasted locusts. Ndama wasn't really hungry, but he could never resist locusts. He took a handful and tossed them into his mouth one by one.

They talked until late and then curled up on the floor to sleep. In the morning their host made some *obusela* and invited them to stay the rest of the day. This Thuku agreed to do, but Ndama insisted that they take him down to the lake and help him find the boat for his return.

"If I were you I wouldn't go back," said Okweli. "Those men over there are pretty wild. While you were asleep Thuku told me about Asila. I would be afraid to go near him. He's a snake!"

"But I promised Bwana Green I would return," protested Ndama.

"What's a promise?" asked Okweli, a cynical smile tugging at the corners of his lips.

"A promise means a lot. I'm a Christian and I keep my word. Have you ever learned to know Jesu Christo?"

Okweli stammered, "I used to go to the mission at Ogada, and I know it's g-good to be a Christian. But if I became one I-I'd have to give up so many things—"

"The only things you need to give up to become a follower of Jesu are the things that harm you. He doesn't want anyone to give up any good thing."

Ndama would have continued, but he could see that it was no use. Okweli knew the way of salvation, but he loved the way of the world.

Thuku and his friend took him to the water's edge and pushed the boat off.

The lake that morning was as calm as water in a basin. There were no clouds, and the trip across to Bwana Green's hut seemed the easiest thing in the world.

Ndama rejoiced in his knowledge of the Lord. He couldn't understand why anyone would think the

Christian life dull or unexciting. He knew of no one who had a more interesting life than he. He dipped his oars into the water and sent the boat scooting forward toward the opposite shore. Thuku had explained that he wouldn't get lost if he continued in the direction he had shown until he could see Chief Mugo's hut. The chief's house was the biggest one around, and Ndama could easily tell it from the others. He knew the place where Bwana Green stayed was just a short distance below it.

He noticed a number of crocodiles swimming nearby, their eyes just out of the water searching for food. Well, he was in the boat and there was no chance for them to get him! The calm water and the cool breeze gave him a wonderful feeling of confidence.

He was worried about Ochella and the missionary, but he knew they were doing the will of the Lord and would be all right. He did hope a mission could be started at the lake for the Luo. He was ever so thankful that Mugo was learning to trust them. In time they could explain the gospel to him, and there was a good possibility that he would accept it. He was already beginning to doubt the magic of Dando.

Rowing on a day like this was a pleasure. He enjoyed every minute of it. A crocodile swam past, and he playfully slapped the water by the monster's tail with the flat side of the oar. The crocodile paid no attention to this. Ndama followed the triangular wake it left in the greenish water and began to sing *More About Jesus* in Olinyore.

Then a wisp of smoke in the distance captured his attention. It curled up into the sky at the place where he believed Chief Mugo's hut to be!

Ndama worked harder at the oars, hoping to get a better view. But the closer he got to the shore, the more certain he became that it was indeed the chief's house. The thoughts of such a tragedy curled the hairs on the back of his neck.

Mugo was about the only friend they had, and he

wasn't completely loyal. Ndama knew how the chief had feared the magic of Dando all his life and he knew it wouldn't be easy to change his thinking in a day or two.

If Mugo's house burned, Ndama knew the blame would be placed on Ochella and himself. A near-panic seized him.

He was now pulling with such speed that every now and then he didn't get the ends of the oars deep enough and they simply skimmed over the water–splashing it into his face. But each mistake simply made him strain harder. He didn't notice his damp shirt. His eyes were glued on the ever increasing spiral of smoke.

Then his feet began to get wet. He assumed that this was because of the water he had clumsily splashed inside with the oars. He continued rowing until water on his ankles caused him to look down. That look forced him to drop the oars, for there was a hole in the bottom of the boat, and water was flooding in!

Quickly he pulled off his shirt, doubled it up and tried to plug the hole which was about three inches across. But this was an impossibility. The hole was too big! There was only one thing to do and that was to start bailing. He picked up the can and started to throw the water out, but he couldn't work fast enough. It covered his ankles and then reached to his shins. He tried to work harder, to stop up the hole with the sole of his foot. But it was no use.

The crocodiles seemed to know what was happening. They swam around the boat, their greedy eyes on Ndama. He could see their crooked, tooth-lined jaws just beneath the water. He prayed for deliverance. The water was now up to his knees, and the sides of the boat were only about five inches above the surface!

The greenish monsters jostled one another, as if they were fighting over who was to get the first bite. The irregular lines between their jaws made it seem as if they were laughing. But Ndama knew this was not so. *Man-*

eaters don't laugh! Hidden in those teeth was all the brutality of the jungle.

He wished he knew how the hole had so mysteriously formed in the boat, but he knew it would never be known. The boat would sink, and if he wasn't eaten he would be drowned like a rat. The sight of the crocodiles made him sick. One of the crocodiles was much bigger than the others, and this one stayed out in front.

Ndama decided that it was useless to bail anymore. The water was coming in ten times as fast as he could scoop it out. The one satisfaction he had was that he knew he had been born again, and that death would simply mean he would go to be with the Lord! Slowly, surely the boat filled; and as it gurgled in, Ndama recognized the gurgle of death.

The water was now up to the edge of the boat; in a moment it would pour in and one of the man-eaters would seize him. He decided that he would leap from the boat before it sank and fool them. This would be sort of a joke, and he might live a few seconds longer. He uttered a prayer of thanks and jumped. Quickly he turned on his back and swam away. The boat, lightened by his escape, rose slightly out of the water.

Trying to swim faster than the crocodiles was an impossibility, but the fear of death spurred him on. With great sweeping strokes he pushed himself forward toward the shore. The largest of the monsters came after him, moving with as little effort as an arrow from a hunting bow.

Ndama tried to make his arms move more quickly, but it was no use. The horrible thing was suddenly by him. It opened its jaws and he felt them close about his waist. This, he thought, was the end. In a moment the other crocodiles would be fighting for him, and then the one that had seized him would swim under the water and he would be drowned. Swiftly he was carried forward. He kept taking deep breaths, never knowing when he would be submerged. The other crocodiles followed, but they could not keep pace with the leader. Soon they were many yards behind. Ndama could feel the dull pressure of the teeth in his flesh. He was certain that in a moment that pressure would be increased and he would be bitten in two!

Then the monster started under. Down, down it went. Ndama held his breath, hoping the crocodile would come to the surface--that some miracle, a charging hippo perhaps, would save him. Pressure built up in his lungs. He felt he couldn't hold his breath a minute longer. Then bright lights leaped into his brain. They seared across his mind like shooting comets. He was aware that he was slowly becoming unconscious. A prayer of desperation formed on his tightly closed lips. Then he began to know that his captor was moving upward toward the surface. His chest was burning with pain. More lights flashed on and off with green and orange and yellow flame. Then, all at once, he felt sunlight in his eyes. He was out of the water again!

He filled his lungs with deep breaths of air, and felt his brain clear. The shore was only a short distance ahead. He wondered what the man-eater was going to do. He prayed that God would help him escape--although he could see no possible way. The forward movement of the crocodile had a tendency to twist his head back, but he was thankful that he was still on top of the water.

The monster headed for a point of land covered with thick clumps of grass and tall papyrus plants. As Ndama watched the approaching land, he wondered if it was the home of some crocodiles, and if he was being taken there to be the main part of a feast. He had heard that crocodiles often did just that sort of thing.

Then the crocodile pushed him through the rough vegetation and laid him on a muddy shelf. Next the twenty-foot reptile backed off a few feet, and then remained motionless--staring at him. Ndama's eyes met the cold eyes of the crocodile. He had a feeling that if he blinked the crocodile would know that he was alive and would proceed to bite him in two!

Ndama had had staring contests with his brother, but he had never won. Long before Ochella's eyes would tire, his would begin to itch, and this would start him to blinking. But now he knew that one blink--one single blink--would bring the crocodile's jaws down on him like a huge pair of pinking shears. It was a terrible thought.

A line of soldier ants began to march across his legs, biting him as they marched. He longed to brush them away, but he could not. Then his nose began to itch and the teeth wounds from the crocodile's jaws began to smart.

The reptile's eyes, like the eyes of Satan, stared at him with no effort at all. It seemed to Ndama that all the evil of the world was coiled deep within them. Suddenly he felt a terrible urge to blink, and he felt certain that he could not stop himself. Silently he prayed for deliverance.

But as he prayed the stare in the eyes became even more intense. Ndama could feel the sweat dripping from his shoulders, and several ants were now biting him at the same time.

Then, just as he knew he would have to give up, the crocodile turned and slithered back into the water.

Instantly Ndama got to his feet and ran for higher ground, for he was certain the monster had just gone to call his friends for the feast. On higher ground, he climbed a tree in order to get his bearings. And then, thanking God, he headed to Bwana Green's hut.

Ndama related the story to the missionary as quickly as possible, mentioning only the main points. When he was through Green said, "If you tell that story to anyone else they won't believe it. But I do because I believe God helped you, and also because the same thing happened to another man about three years ago. Only this other man wasn't as fortunate as you, for the crocodile placed him on a tiny island and he had to wait for three days before he could get a boat to stop and rescue him!”

The missionary then dressed his wounds and gave him a new shirt. Ochella made a pot of *obusuma* and Ndama ate greedily.

After he had rested for an hour or so Green came into the hut and sat down beside him. “I wish this were the end of our troubles,” he said. “But it isn’t. Our troubles are just beginning. Mugo’s house burned and Dando is blaming it onto Ochella!”

“Well, did you do it?” asked Ndama, twisting his eyes around for a full view of his younger brother.

“Of course not!” snapped Ochella in an offended tone.

“I was just teasing,” soothed Ndama with a big smile.

“I heard a rumor that the Luo are going to come and get us,” continued Green seriously.

“Won’t Chief Mugo stop them?” asked Ndama.

“That’s just it. I think he believes it is true,” said Green. “He didn’t come today for his eye treatment!”

“I think we’d better get out of here and return to Bunyore,” put in Ochella.

“I wouldn’t think of such a thing,” said Ndama warmly. “God has called us, and....”

His sentence was cut in two by a loud knock at the door.

Green unbolted it to look out, and at that moment it was pushed wide open and a Luo thrust his face inside. “We’ve come to get you,” he announced.

A big crowd of armed warriors outside chanted, “Get them, get them, get them!”

Before the brothers could protest they were dragged outside and their hands tied behind their backs. Green, too, was tied in the same fashion. Then they were marched down to the lake. Chief Mugo followed close behind, and Ndama could tell that his heart was full of hate.

7   Accused

AS THEY WERE being forced down the path that led to the lake Ndama noticed Dando watched him curiously. He wondered about this because every time he looked at the witch doctor the old man shifted his eyes to someone else. He was also puzzled to know why the fire had been blamed on Ochella. Usually he was the one blamed for any serious mischief.

"We are now going to throw you to the crocodiles," announced Dando importantly.

"Before you do that we want to see if they are really guilty," said Chief Mugo after he had taken a place by the medicine man. "I believe in justice, and as long as I'm chief we're going to have it!"

"Do you not believe they should be thrown to the crocodiles?" demanded Dando.

"I believe in justice," replied Mugo firmly.

The witch doctor smiled widely at the chief. Then as he fingered the tiny bones in the spinal column tied around his neck he said, "Anyone who would burn the beautiful house of our wonderful chief deserves to be thrown to the crocodiles." He pointed a crafty finger at a dozen of the man-eating monsters sunning themselves at the water's edge. "See," he added dramatically, "even the crocodiles know we should throw them into the lake!"

As he spoke three of the twenty-foot monsters pushed themselves into the water and swam away.

"No one will do a thing unless we know they are guilty," countered the chief firmly.

"I, myself, am convinced of their guilt," said Dando. "With my own eyes I saw Ochella light a match and put it to the roof. A man's ears are sometimes mistaken, but never his eyes!"

Ochella started to say something, but Ndama whispered to him to keep still.

"I agree that if they burned the house they should be given to the crocodiles," said Mugo. "But I'm still not convinced."

"Do you mean I'm a liar?" asked Dando angrily.

"No, I just mean that we are going to have justice," repeated Mugo, his eyes lighting up with determination.

"Neither Ochella nor I were near Chief Mugo's house when it burned," said Ndama. "We did not come to the land of the Luo to burn houses. We came to teach you about Jesu Christo and how He died to save sinners!"

He swept his eyes over the crowd of forty or fifty men, searching for a look of mercy on their black faces. But there was none. Even though Mugo had been arguing for justice his face was hard with cruel lines around his smoke-filled eyes and thick lips.

"Quiet!" shouted Dando. "Boys who go around burning houses deserve to die. Bunyore boys are no good. They are just like their fathers. Years ago, before the white men came, we used to spear the Bunyore and take their cattle. And this was the easiest thing there was. It was just like going to a store. The Bunyories are weaker than shadows!"

"The fire was burning when I was out on the lake, and Ochella was in the hut with Bwana Green," said Ndama.

"If this is so someone would have seen you," sneered

Dando. He turned to the crowd. "Did any of you see them in these places?" he asked, a smile of contempt playing about his white-streaked lips.

The men all shook their heads, and one young fellow with an extra-long spear in his hand said, "No, we didn't see them."

Ndama swallowed hard as he noticed the way the witch doctor was influencing Mugo. "It is true," he gulped, "that the Luo and the Bunyore have speared each other for years. You burned our villages, and we burned yours; you took our cattle, and we took yours. But I always felt that you were a fair people—that you would never punish anyone without a trial!"

"The boy is right," said Mugo. "We won't punish anyone without a trial!"

"All right," said Dando confidently, "you'll have a trial." He motioned to a young man who was learning to become a witch doctor. "Go grind up some flour," he directed. "Make it very fine. We will give them the flour test. It will show their guilt and make the crocodiles happy!"

"Let's try to run," urged Ochella.

"That's impossible," exclaimed Ndama.

A hippopotamus came to the surface less than a bowshot away. There was a baby hippo on her back. The mother eyed the crowd sullenly, twitched her tiny pink ears and sank beneath the waves without a ripple.

"There is only one thing that will save us," whispered Ndama, "and that is not to be afraid when they give us the test."

"But how can we keep from being afraid?" asked Ochella, pointing with his lips to the hungry crocodiles.

"Our hope is in the Lord. Remember the 23rd Psalm?"

"I will fear no evil: for thou art with me...," quoted Ochella.

Dando approached with a handful of the finely

ground flour. "I'm going to put this into each one of your mouths," he said. "If you swallow it we'll let you go; but if it blows out your mouths we'll know you're guilty and throw you to the crocodiles!"

Ndama faced the crowd. "This is an old test," he said bravely. "It was used in Bunyore many years ago, and I believe it is a good test. It tells when people are lying. For when they are lying they are afraid and there is no saliva in their mouths, and they can't swallow flour. But if they have been telling the truth they have enough saliva to dampen the flour and thus swallow it. Ochella and I have been telling the truth, and we'll swallow the flour without any trouble. That means you will have to set us free. But after we've been freed I think *others* should take the test!"

The witch doctor scowled at this. "Prisoners don't make decisions," he grumbled. "It is the chief who will decide what we'll do. Anyway the boys will…"

"He is right," interrupted the chief, speaking loud enough for all to hear. "If they are not guilty we will search until we find the guilty one, and when we find him we'll throw him to the crocodiles!"

Presently a large half-gourd heaped high with flour was given to the chief.

"Now, I want all the warriors and Dando to come and test the flour, for we want to be honest," said Mugo.

The men got in line. Then each one picked up a handful of flour and let it slowly sift through his fingers. Ndama shuddered as he watched them, for most of their fingers were filthy. But the flour passed the test.

"It is very fine," said one of them. "My woman could never grind flour like that, and it is much too fine for our food. But it is just what we need for the test."

"Now let me repeat what we are going to do," said Dando, "for, like Mugo, I want to be fair."

He waited until everyone was listening, and then he went on. "We will fill each of the boys' mouths with flour.

If he can swallow it we will know he is innocent, but if he can't we will know he is guilty and we will then throw him to the crocodiles. Does everyone understand?"

"Kweli! Kweli! We all understand," they chanted back.

"All right, then, boys," he smirked, "open your mouths and face the crocodiles."

The witch doctor stuffed the boys' mouths full of flour, and then stood off at a distance and sneered at them. "Chew it well," he exhorted, his arms smugly folded on his chest. "The crocodiles are hungry!"

The warriors crowded around to see how the boys would make out. "They'll never swallow it," said one.

"Let's wait and see," said another, his face within a few inches of Ochella's.

As Ndama closed his lips over the flour a surge of terror shot through his body. What if he couldn't get it down? The thought made his knees sag. Then he prayed more earnestly than he had ever prayed before: "Lord, drive away my fears; don't let Satan scare me."

Instantly a calmness came over him, and he felt the flour turn into a lump in his mouth. The lump was a big one, and he had to bite it and swallow five times before he got it down. When the last part dropped down his throat tears of happiness squeezed from his eyes. Then he opened his mouth to the witch doctor.

Dando peered inside—then his face became more ferocious than before. "It's just a trick," he exclaimed viciously. "He didn't really swallow it!"

"Look in Ochella's mouth, before you speak again," said Mugo, his voice crisp with authority.

Ochella opened his mouth and Dando looked inside. "The flour is g-gone but I kn-know he didn't swallow it," he wailed.

The chief then went up to the boys and examined their mouths. He poked his finger inside their cheeks and asked them to spit on the ground.

The boys spat on the ground as the chief instructed, and there wasn't a particle of flour in their spittle.

"Cut them loose, and cut Bwana Green loose," commanded Mugo, "and grind up some more flour!"

"Don't let them go just yet," objected Dando crisply.

"Why not?" demanded Mugo.

"Because—because they have just played a trick on us. They didn't really swallow the flour!" said Dando.

"Then where is it?" demanded the chief.

"I-I d–don't know," sputtered the witch doctor. "But I think we should give them another kind of a test. We don't want to make a mistake—a mistake that could cause more houses to be burned. When there is a snake in the village everyone has to be careful. Is that not true?" he asked, gesturing to the crowd.

"*Kweli! Kweli!*" they answered.

"These boys have been going to the white man's school," continued the witch doctor craftily, "and they have changed some of their ways. When I looked inside their mouths I noticed that neither of them had his six lower front teeth removed, and as everyone knows a Bunyore or a Jaluo who keeps his front teeth is a coward and looks like a goat. That's true, isn't it?"

"*Kweli! Kweli!*" shouted the crowd.

"Also, I notice that neither of them have tattooed their faces, and this makes them look almost as bad as the white man. That's true, isn't it?"

"*Kweli! Kweli!*"

"And those who've watched them have seen how they try to help the white man—the man who is our enemy, for his brothers make us pay taxes and they lock our friends in the Kisumu jail. This is terrible, isn't it?"

"*Kweli! Kweli!* It is very bad!"

"Now these boys are going to the white man's school," went on Dando, pushing out his chest and filling his voice with sarcasm. "Do you not think it would be wise for us to have them show us one thing they have learned—one thing that would be of value to our people?”

"*Kweli! Kweli!* We should do that.”

“You have spoken words of wisdom,” said Mugo. “Let the boys show us one thing they know that is of value. This is important, for already I have heard of some young people that want to go to their school.”

“It is now time for us to go home and eat,” said Dando. “Let us return when the sun has gone to bed and the stars are out. And then, as Ndama stands in front of the fire he can show us the value of the white man’s school.”

With his back to the log fire, Ndama felt every eye from the secret society peering at him. The hatred in the stares was so intense he squirmed and prayed silently for help.

“We are all here,” sneered Dando. “Now tell us what you learned in school. Our ears are open.”

Ndama searched their faces, and hesitated. He licked his dry lips as he wondered what he should say.

“Go on, tell us something,” chided Dando. “If you can’t think of anything else you might tell us how you learned to burn people’s houses!”

“I learned many things at school,” began Ndama. “But the best thing I learned is that Jesu Christo is a true friend—that He helps at all times. He changed my ways and gave me a clean heart. And He can do the same—”

“We don’t want to hear about the white man’s religion,” shouted Dando, getting up and stamping his feet. “We want to know if you learned anything that would help our people. We are fighting for *Uhuru* (independence). We will have our own government. We need wisdom that will make us strong.”

Months before, as the hyenas howled in the Bunyore Hills, Ndama had tossed on his bed and had wondered what he would do if he faced an occasion like this. Now, even though his legs were wobbly, he was prepared.

Quickly he whipped a Swahili New Testament from his khaki jacket, and read: *"Kwanihivyo ndivyo, Mungu alivyoupenda ulimwengo…* (For God so loved the world…)."

"Don't read another word!" shouted Dando. "We don't want to hear about the new religion."

"But can't you see how I know what the white leaves are saying?" asked Ndama. "Can any of you do that?"

"No! No, we don't want to learn to sit and stare at white leaves as we've seen you and others doing," said Dando. "We're men, not women!"

"Maybe others would like to hear what the book says," suggested Ndama, hopefully.

"No, Dando is right," said Mugo, adjusting his red fez. "There is a hunchback from Luanda who often comes down here and tells people about Jesu Christo. But our ears are closed to this religion, for we have heard that if one follows Jesu he can only have one wife and that he has to quit drinking. We will only listen to you when you show us something that you can do better than any of us…"

"Yes, that's right," agreed a young man on the edge of the crowd. "Show us something that is useful."

Ndama's mind raced over the things he had learned. What could he do better than anyone else? It must be something the Jaluo could understand. He was very good at arithmetic; but there was no way of demonstrating this. He had also learned nearly five hundred words of English. This, however, would be of little concern to these people. Then he remembered he had won the spear and hoop competition on the last day of school.

"Send out word that tomorrow when the sun is halfway down the sky we'll have a spear and hoop contest," said Ndama. "I'll show you how to throw a spear!"

"Being able to throw a spear properly is most important," approved Mugo, "for one must always be prepared to meet a hyena, a leopard or even a python. But I'm surprised that you'd learn anything about spear-throwing at the white man's school. A white man can't throw a spear. All he can do is shoot a *bunduki!*"

"If you win the competition," scoffed Dembu, "I'll let you read to me about Jesu Christo for a whole day." He hacked and spat into the fire to show his scorn. "I'm going to invite my friend Onyamba to come. He can throw a spear quicker than a black mamba can strike."

The crowd that gathered for the hoop and spear contest was much larger than Ndama had expected, and the entire crowd with the exception of Ochella and Bwana Green was for Onyamba.

Swallowing hard, Ndama addressed the crowd. "I think all of us know what to do. But to be certain, I'll mention the rules again. The hoop will be rolled across the meadow, and while it is rolling each contestant will try to throw his spear through it. The one who pins it down will mark the place on the grass where he stood when he threw his spear. Then the others will throw their spears from that spot—each one trying to make his spear stick in the ground inside the hoop. Every time a spear misses, the one who snared the hoop gets a point."

In a moment, the hoop made of slender osiola limbs bound together with banana tree bark, came rolling down the grass. The hoop, about the size of a truck tire, was a rather difficult target—especially since it didn't always roll straight. A dozen spears were thrown. Each one missed by a wide margin. Then Onyamba, standing farther away than anyone, threw his spear and pinned the hoop neatly to the ground.

He marked the spot where he had been standing by grinding a heel into the soft turf. "Well, there it is," he said with a swagger. "Remember each time you miss I get a point!"

When Ndama went up to throw he was crowded out by others; and as each one threw, the spear went wild. Dando laughed at each miss and shouted, "See,

Onyamba is the best spear thrower in all of the world." He counted each miss with a jeering voice, *"Moja–mbili–tatu–nne–tano–sita–nane–tisa–kumi–"*

Finally Ndama was allowed to take his place. It seemed to him that the others were missing on purpose–missing so that their man could score.

"Do you want me to say some magic words?" asked Dando, as Ndama drew his arm back for the throw.

Ndama felt a stab of anger as the medicine man spoke, and was tempted to accuse the others of cheating. But he knew if he did this he would be scorned by the crowd and it would hinder his accuracy. He kept his temper by quietly praying and quoting the books of the New Testament under his breath. *"Mateo–Marko–Luka–Yohana–Matendo ya Mitumi–Barua ya Paulo Kwa Waroma."*

"Hurry up and throw your spear," chided Mugo. "Don't just stand there like a sick stork!"

Quickly Ndama drew back his arm and threw, and the spear went straight into the center of the hoop. "Well, that is that," he said proudly. "Now I want you to throw the hoop for me."

The hoop roller picked it up and was in the act of rolling it across the meadow when Ndama stopped him. "You haven't taken it far enough away," he said. "Take it right to the edge of the meadow."

As the man with the hoop kept moving over, the crowd shook their heads.

"What a boaster he is!" jeered one.

"Who has ever speared a hoop that far?" asked another.

"We'll see about that," replied Ndama, rubbing his hands in the dirt in order to rid them of sweat.

"The school boy–the follower of the new religion, the one who is afraid to have his teeth pulled–is now going to show us something new," sneered Onyamba. "Well, we've laughed before and we will laugh again."

While they scoffed Ndama prayed silently for special

strength. He knew that it would be very easy to miss, and that the hoop was really quite far away. But with all the points Onyamba had made by having his friends deliberately miss, he knew he would have to spear it at a great distance. For a moment he shut his eyes in prayer, and then he walked over to the proper throwing area. Then, turning to Dando, he said, "Maybe you had better make some magic that will cause my spear to miss, for if I snare the hoop from this distance I will win."

"I don't need to make magic," snapped Dando, "for no one could spear the hoop at that distance."

"All right, roll the hoop," said Ndama, getting braced.

He waited for the hoop to pass directly in front, and then with his hand firmly on the haft, he took three forward steps and threw.

The spear arched upward, higher and higher. Ndama held his breath as it seemed to hover in the air. He had aimed in front of the hoop, and now he was afraid he had miscalculated the distance. But no, his aim was right and the hoop was securely prisoned to the ground!

Quickly Ndama whirled on his heel at the spot where he had stood when he threw the spear. Now all you have to do," he said proudly, "is to put one spear into the hoop and the game will be over. Dando will count every spear that misses. With him counting, no one will be able to cheat. Is that true?"

"Kweli! Kweli! That is true," roared the crowd with approval.

Soon a line of contestants was formed and their spears began to arch toward the hoop. Onyamba tried six different times, but he couldn't even get close.

"Well, it seems that I know how to do at least one thing that is helpful," said Ndama.

"Yes, you have shown your wisdom and the strength of your arm," said Mugo. "We are ready now to do you a favor. Do you have a request?"

"Yes, I have one request," said Ndama slowly and

deliberately. "I am most unhappy about the way Chief Mugo's house was burned, and I think that we should find the man who set the fire."

"*Kweli! Kweli!* We should find him," approved the crowd with enthusiasm.

"Since Dando insisted that Ochella and I take the flour test, I believe that he should also take it," continued Ndama.

"But I don't have time to take it," stammered Dando. "I have been called to see a very sick man in another village."

"Oh, yes you do," said Mugo, laying a hand on his shoulder. "The test won't take very long, and if you are innocent you should not be afraid to take it."

"But I must go," insisted Dando.

"You can go after you've passed the test," said Mugo firmly. "And if you don't pass the test you will be thrown to the crocodiles!"

When the flour was ready, the crowd gathered around while Mugo placed it in the witch doctor's mouth. Dando tried to chew it, but his mouth was as dry as the hard granite stones that cover the Bunyore Hills. The flour blew from his lips in tiny puffs.

Suddenly Dando whirled on the crowd: "If you don't leave this moment I will put a curse on you that will fill your heads with lizards," he threatened.

But instead of leaving, the crowd merely laughed.

"You fooled us before," said one of the older men, "but you will not fool us again."

"That's right," added Chief Mugo. "You tried to cure my eyes and failed, but Bwana White Man has already made them much better."

Dando sank to his knees. "Please–please, Chief Mugo," he whimpered, "have mercy on me! I burned your house; but I will build you a bigger and better one, and I'll give you all my cows. Please!"

"Bind him!" cut in Mugo angrily. "Bind him and

throw him to the crocodiles!"

"Kweli! Kweli!" chanted the crowd. "He should be bound and fed to the crocodiles. He has already caused too much trouble!"

The witch doctor tried to run away, but he was tripped by one of the younger men and fell sprawling on his face. In a moment his hands were placed behind him and securely tied with sisal rope.

"I'll put a curse on you!" he snarled as he was being led to the crocodiles.

"We're not afraid of your curses anymore," said Chief Mugo, leading the way to the green monsters at the very edge of the lake. "Our eyes have been opened and we have taken our fingers out of our ears. From now on we are going to listen to Ndama and Ochella and Bwana Green."

Suddenly Ndama barred the way to the lake. "Stop!" he shouted. "Stop! Please, I don't want Dando thrown to the crocodiles."

"Why not?" demanded the chief, his chest heaving with anger.

"Because I'm a Christian, and Christians do good to those who've harmed them."

Mugo's eyes widened. "You mean you want to save his life after all he's done to you?"

Ndama nodded.

The chief scratched his head in amazement. Then he said, "Bring Dando back. Ndama has just shown me something that is really wonderful. He wants to spare the witch doctor's life! The kind of religion that will do this is a good religion. I want Ndama and Ochella to come to our village. We'll make a feast for them, and then we'll listen while they talk about this friend of theirs, Jesu Christo. Let all who are agreed clap their hands."

The crowd clapped their hands as one man. Then the chief said, "We won't throw Dando to the crocodiles, but we will have him put in the Kisumu jail–and when

Bwana D. C. learns what kind of man he's been he'll keep him there for a long time."

"Before you take him," said Ndama, "I want to ask him a question." He went over to the men holding the prisoner, and after the crowd had quieted, said, "I want to know how that hole was made in the bottom of the boat Thuku and I used."

"I don't know anything about it," replied Dando sullenly.

"Are you sure? asked Ndama.

"Of course I'm sure!" said the witch doctor angrily.

8   End of Mystery

T HE MAIN THING that worries me is that hole in the boat," said Ndama after he'd swallowed a big mouthful of *obusuma*.

"There's no use thinking about that," replied Ochella. "You're here. The boat's at the bottom of the lake, and so-"

"I know that," cut in Ndama impatiently. "But I'd like to know who did it, and how they did it. I really thought Thuku had become a Christian. I'd hate to think he'd do such a thing, and yet it seems he did! I believe Dando knows, but refuses to tell. When I asked him he had such a peculiar look on his face."

"Let's be happy we have a chance to preach tomorrow," said Green. "This is a most wonderful opportunity."

"I'm very glad for the way things have turned," persisted Ndama. "But I'm still curious to know who played such a mean trick. I might have been eaten by one of those crocodiles. You should have seen their teeth!"

The feast was a big one. There were hundreds of people present and there was plenty of food. Big pots of bananas, *obusuma* and fish boiled over the little fires built for them. The chief had butchered his largest cow, and generous slices of meat were being roasted and boiled. Dozens of wide plates were loaded down with *obusuma*, and there was a big basket full of roasted locusts for Ndama and Ochella.

One of the men had worked for a European in Nairobi and he was employed to make a special meal for Bwana Green. A long wooden table was brought from a nearby village and set under a banana tree for the missionary. There were no knives or forks in the village, but Ndama had brought Green's along and these were used. The cook had fried a large omelet, using twenty-seven eggs, and had made a roast out of the cow's hump for the white man.

The Luo went after their food greedily. Saying grace before meals was something they had never heard of. When Bwana Green bowed his head in thanks, they were mystified. Ndama and Ochella ate and ate and then rubbed their stomachs so they could eat some more. When everyone was finished a basin of water was passed around for the guests to wash their hands in. Green merely washed his hands, but the Luo washed their hands, and then scooped some of the water into their mouths and rinsed them out.

Then Mugo got to his feet. "I used to hate all the white people," he said. "But I have learned that Bwana Green is a fine man. When I went to him with my sick eyes he started putting *dowa* in them. They are now almost well. He hasn't asked me to pay him even a little chicken. Dando also tried to make my eyes well. I gave him four goats, a cow and seven chickens but he did no good. I think Bwana White Man's medicine is much stronger than that of the witch doctor.

"Another thing I noticed is that Bwana White Man has a thunderstick. When he pointed it at the hippo it made so much noise the animal died. He could have pointed this stick of death at us, but he didn't. He says that he loves us and I believe it. I've asked him to speak to us and tell what it is that makes him and Ndama and Ochella so full of love and bravery."

Using Ndama as an interpreter Bwana Green told the crowd how much he enjoyed the meal, and then he began to preach to them. He explained how God had made the world and all the people, and how men had fallen into sin. As he was emphasizing that all men have sinned Mugo got to his feet. "Do you mean that everyone who ever lived has fallen into the sharp trap of sin?"

"Yes," replied Green, "everyone, with the exception of Jesus Christ, who is God's only Son, has sinned."

"I knew Dando was a sinner," said Mugo, "but I didn't know that everyone else had sinned, too."

"It is sin that cuts us off from God," continued Green. "When a man sins he deserves to die. I know you know this because when you found the witch doctor out you wanted to throw him to the crocodiles. But we don't have to die as a result of our sins because Jesu Christo died for us instead."

Mugo jumped to his feet. "I don't understand why He should die for us," he complained, his eyes widening.

"What do you do when you catch a thief?" asked Green.

"We make him take back what he stole and pay a fine or go to jail in Kisumu," replied a voice from the crowd.

"Let us suppose, then," said Green, "that a man is asked to pay a fine, but the fine is too big for him to pay. What does he do?"

"He then has to go to jail," replied a dozen people all at the same time.

"But suppose that I would come along and learn what the fine was and pay it for him. What would you do then?"

"We'd have to let him go," returned Mugo.

"Well, that is what Jesu Christo has done for us," said Green with a big smile, for the natives were beginning to understand. "He allowed men to nail Him on a cross. He died there, and His death pays the price of all our sins."

"Even Dando's?" asked Mugo.

"Yes, even Dando's!" replied Green. "But we must remember that even though our sins have been paid for, they are not forgiven unless we accept the price Jesu Christo paid."

"I don't understand, Bwana White Man," said Mugo, his brows knitted together in a puzzled frown.

"Do you remember that I told you about a man who was asked to pay a fine that was too big for him to pay?"

The crowd nodded.

"Do you remember I said that I could come along and pay it for him?"

They nodded again, and one man said, "Truly, that is what we heard."

"Now, before you'd let the man go he'd have to pay the fine. But suppose even though I offer to pay it for him he refuses?"

"Then he'd have to go to jail," said Mugo with enthusiasm.

"It is that way in this matter of sin," continued Green. "Jesu Christo paid the price of all our sins, but before this can possibly help us we must accept the gift!"

"I'm beginning to understand!" exclaimed Mugo, his eyes dancing.

"Those who want their sins forgiven must tell the Lord they are sinners. If they have stolen they should return what they have taken, and if they can't return it all at once they should return it as soon as possible. If they have lied about someone they must correct those lies. And then they must believe that Jesu Christo died to pay the price of their sins. His death will not help those who refuse to believe."

He leafed through his New Testament until he came to the tenth chapter of Romans and the ninth verse. "This book," he said, holding it up for all to see, "is the Word of

God. It is full of messages to us, and whatever it says is true. I'm going to read one of the short messages God has given us, and I'll ask Ndama to interpret it to you." He then read, "That if thou shalt confess with thy mouth the Lord Jesus, and shalt believe in thine heart that God hath raised him from the dead, thou shalt be saved."

"That sounds wonderful," said Mugo a little sadly, "but that must be just for white people. All of us know that because the white man has a gun he has been able to take everything."

"Oh, listen, Mugo," said Bwana Green. "I want you to know that anyone can be saved. The color of the person's skin doesn't matter at all. If you will do the things that this book says, Jesu Christo will forgive your sins and give you a new heart. He will make you love the things that are good and hate the things that are bad. He did all of this for Ndama and Ochella, and I'll ask them to tell you about it right now."

Ndama and Ochella gave their testimonies, and the crowd shook their heads in wonder. Then Mugo angrily got to his feet. "Why didn't you tell us this a long time ago?" he demanded. "Anyone who knows such good news and keeps it a secret should be thrown to the crocodiles!"

"We wish we could have come a long time ago," explained Green, "but we had to go to other places first. There are hundreds of villages and tribes in Africa where the people have never heard these things."

Mugo and his friends would not let the missionary go. Green and the brothers stayed and preached to them for nearly a week, and at the end of this time Mugo and thirteen others had become Christians.

When it was time for Green to return to Bunyore, Mugo held his hand and wouldn't let it go until the missionary promised to send them a teacher. At first Green had said, "I'll have one sent to you next year." But this didn't satisfy the chief.

"We want a man now," he insisted. Finally Green

said, "I'll do all I can to get you a teacher right away."

The mystery of the hole in the bottom of the boat was still unsolved, and Ndama kept searching for the solution. He hoped that it was someone other than Thuku.

On their last day in the hut Thuku came in. At first Ndama didn't recognize him for he was dressed in a trim white shirt and khaki trousers.

"Where have you been?" demanded Ndama.

"My friend in Kisumu got me a job, and since I wanted to buy these new clothes I took it. The job was a good one and I ate (was paid) twelve shillings. I even have three shillings left!"

Ndama related the boat story, and watched him curiously to see if he had a guilty conscience. But if he did he didn't reveal it. "I can't even think of a person who would do such a horrible deed unless it would be Dando or Asila," said Thuku.

"The part I can't understand," said Ndama, "is that the hole was in the boat on my return trip. If it had been there on the way to Kisumu I would have believed that it was the witch doctor. But everything was all right on the way over—"

"I suppose it looks like I was the one," replied Thuku, shaking his head. "But I'm a Christian and I wouldn't even think of such a thing!"

"Who else could have done it?" asked Ochella from the back of the hut.

"I don't know," sighed Thuku, throwing out his hands in a gesture of despair.

Ndama changed the subject by telling Thuku about the meeting with Mugo and his friends. He seemed overjoyed at the news, and when he learned there might be some delay in getting a missionary he was annoyed. He took the three shillings out of his pocket and gave them to Green. "Maybe these will help to get a teacher," he said.

As the boys packed, Ochella said, "Wouldn't it be wonderful if Father would become a Christian?"

"But he's been a rainmaker for so many years. That's how he makes a living. He is very stubborn about changing his mind."

The boys continued to pack until noon. Ndama's mind was still wondering how the hole had gotten into the boat. Bwana Green took his place behind the wheel and was in the act of driving off when a young man motioned for him to stop.

"What do you want?" asked the missionary, after he had turned off the key.

"My name is Ndombe," panted the slender young man, for he had been running. "I'm the one who went with you to get the hippo. Remember?"

"How could I ever forget!" exclaimed Ndama. "No one can forget the day he nearly died."

"I-I have something I w-want to tell you," said Ndombe, nervously digging a hole in the sand with his big toe.

"Go ahead and tell us," encouraged Ndama. "We are listening."

"It is about the new religion."

"Yes, go on," said Ndama.

"I heard what you had to say about Jesu Christo, and I've noticed a big change in Thuku and Mugo. I-I also w-want to become a Ch-Christian."

"That's wonderful!" exclaimed Ndama.

"But before I can become a follower of Jesu I must make a confession," said Ndombe, his eyes on the ground.

"Well, we are here all by ourselves," said Green gently. "What is it that you would like to confess?"

"My confession is very hard," said Ndombe. "Right now, while I'm trying to speak my mouth is as dry as an old bone and my heart is full of fear–"

"You don't need to be afraid," said Ochella. "We are your friends, and we will do all we can to help you."

"I-I'm the o-one who cut the hole in the bottom of the boat. I cut out a large piece with a little saw I borrowed from an Indian. Then I glued it back in. I did this so that the glue would melt in the middle of the lake and the boat would sink. Dando is the one who made me do it. I-I'm v-very s-sorry." The words came from his mouth in a flood, like water over a falls. By the time he had finished he was trembling and there were tears in his eyes.

"Ndombe," said Ndama, putting an arm around the Jaluo's waist, "I have forgiven you, and I know that Jesu Christo has forgiven you, for He has promised to do just that in His Book. Now you must tell Jesu Christo that you are a sinner and that you believe He died to pay the price of your sins. Have you done that?"

"Yes, Ndama, I have."

"Then," continued Ndama, "let us all kneel right here in front of the truck and thank God for giving you the gift of salvation."

The four of them knelt by the truck, and Ndombe joined the others in a prayer of thanksgiving. And then he got on his feet, his face shining.

"My, I feel as light as a piece of paper," he said. "It is certainly wonderful to be a Christian!"

9 The Wonderful Toothache

NDAMA AND OCHELLA'S father, Libuki, was extremely glad to welcome them back to Bunyore. He listened to their stories with great pride, even though he was not a Christian. But one evening as the three of them sat by the smoldering fire at the edge of their village, he said, "Ndama, you and Ochella have had wonderful adventures. But I have decided that you cannot work with Bwana Green anymore."

"Why not?" asked Ndama, thoroughly alarmed.

"There are many reasons, Ndama," replied Libuki, thoughtfully rubbing his chin. "One of the reasons is that I am a rainmaker, and Bwana White Man tells people that I am a fraud–that I can't really make it rain.

"Now both of you know that my only way of eating shillings is by making it rain when the skies are stubborn. That's how I get money to pay taxes and buy the cows you will use when you want to get a wife."

"But Bwana Green is our friend!" exclaimed Ochella. "He has never done us any harm, and he has never tried to stop you from making it rain."

"You are still boys," said Libuki, getting up and stretching his arms. "You just don't understand. Bwana Green is my enemy. I forbid you to ever work with him again!"

Ndama bit his lower lip as he watched his father disappear into the shadows. He knew that if Libuki said no he meant no, and that it would be almost impossible to change his mind.

For several years Libuki had thought better of the missionary. He had allowed Ndama and Ochella to go to the Day of Rest School, to go with Green on long safaris, and to work with him at the mission. But now he was losing some of his trade because those who went to school learned that he really could not make it rain.

"Well, what can we do now?" asked Ochella glumly.

"I-I don't know," shrugged Ndama; "but I know God will help us think of a way to get Father to change his mind. Let's not worry about that now. Both of us need to have our heads shaved, and so let's do that while we think. I'll shave yours and you can shave mine."

Ndama filled a gourd dipper in the back of the hut with water, and then placed Ochella on a three-legged stool outside in the fierce sunlight. His and Ochella's kinky hair had not been shaved since they had gone with Bwana Green to Kisumu. It was now over an inch long.

"Could you think of something we could do to change Father's mind?" said Ndama, as he dipped the old razor blade into the water and shaved a narrow path through Ochella's hair.

"I can't think of a single thing," said Ochella, squirming away from the razor when it pulled. "Father can be as stubborn as a black-faced bull!"

"Perhaps if we did something that would fill his heart with joy we might be able to change his mind. When Father is glad he is really generous," said Ndama.

"Maybe we could make him something especially good to eat," said Ochella.

"Like what?"

"Well, he is especially fond of *wimbe obusuma* and boiled meat taken from the hump of a cow."

"But where would we get the *wimbe* flour?"

"We have a basket of *wimbe* in the back of our hut," said Ochella.

"But we can't make *obusuma* out of the *wimbe* unless it is ground. Can you grind it?"

"No, I can't grind flour. I'm not a woman!" exclaimed Ochella. "But maybe Chuma, the daughter of Baku, the witch doctor, would grind it for us. She's a wonderful Christian, and she's helped us before."

The boys finished shaving each other's heads and then they went over to Chuma's hut.

"Of course I'll grind it for you," said Chuma. "But if I do, you'll have to take care of my little brother Tuti while I do it."

"Of course we'll help you," promised Ochella, taking the chubby little boy outside into the yard that surrounded the hut.

Chuma placed the wicker basket filled with *wimbe* by the side of the long flat grinding stone. Then she poured out a handful of the little red grains on top of the stone, and began to grind them by rubbing a smaller stone on top of them as they rolled down from their perch on the end of the bigger stone. It took a lot of skill to do this, but Chuma was an expert. She had been grinding ever since she had lost her baby teeth.

"Be careful and don't get any bits of stone into the flour," warned Ndama. "If Father bites on a grain of sand or a bit of rock he will be so angry he'll never even let us go to the Day of Rest School."

"Don't worry about me," laughed Chuma, her pretty face shining with sweat. "But if you're going to make a meal that will really make your father's heart glad, you had better hurry into Luanda and get the meat."

Ochella agreed to stay with Tuti while Ndama went to the market for the meat.

"Be sure and get a good piece," said Chuma. "If you get one big enough so that I can have some, I'll cook the food for you!"

Back at his hut, Ndama selected a chicken to trade for the meat; and then he set out for Luanda, the chicken squawking under his arm.

The market that day was crowded with all kinds of traders. Dozens of wrinkled old women were sitting on the ground with their wares before them. Some had little packages of rock salt wrapped in brown banana leaves; others, tall quail baskets made of twisted papyrus rope; and still others, three-legged stools, beads, pipestems and bracelets.

Ndama walked by all of the traders, muttering a word of greeting to each one as he passed, and headed over to the place where a bull had been butchered. Here, after much haggling, he traded his chicken for the firm hump off the bull's back. This was a favorite piece, for it was very tender and without any bones.

"Now, Chuma," advised Ndama, "we want you to make the best *obusuma* that you have ever made, and do a good job with the meat. The hardness of our father's heart depends on you!"

"I will do my best," promised Chuma with a big smile that revealed her even, white teeth. "But really, *obusuma* cannot change a man's heart. The only one who can do that is God. All three of us ought to pray about it. God will answer prayer. I know!"

After prayer, Chuma filled a pot with water and placed it on the three stones in the center of the floor. Then she built a fire between the stones. Next, after the water had started to boil, she poured in the red *wimbe* flour, allowing it to sift through her fingers while she stirred the water.

She kept adding flour until the paste-like *obusuma* was too stiff to stir. Then she placed it in a wicker basket and smoothed it down with a paddle until it was round and firm like a grinding stone.

Next she helped Ndama cut the meat into tiny pieces

and boil it with a pinch of salt they had purchased in Luanda a month before.

After the careful preparations were completed, Ndama and Ochella carried the delicious meal back to their hut. When they arrived, Libuki was sitting on a stool in front of the hut.

"Mirembe, Father," greeted Ndama gaily, "we have brought you some good food that will make your stomach happy."

Libuki looked at the *wimbe obusuma.* "This is my favorite food," he said, taking a handful and working it in his hand until it was just the right size to fit in his mouth.

He chewed the food thoughtfully. Then, with a cunning look in his eyes, he asked, "Why have you cooked all of this for me?"

"Because we love you!" replied Ndama and Ochella almost together. "We were gone from you for a long, long time and we didn't want you to think that we had forgotten you. You and Mother are still our favorite persons!"

Libuki ate and ate. He smacked his lips and Ndama's hopes began to rise. His father was in a good mood. Soon he would be rubbing his stomach and saying, *"Cupa cupa* (yum yum)." The moment he did this, Ndama decided, he would ask for permission to work with Bwana Green again.

Breathlessly Ndama watched as his father took bigger and bigger handfuls of *obusuma* while he exclaimed, *"Cupa cupa, cupa cupa.* My, this is good food. If you can get wives who can cook like this you will be fortunate even though you have to pay ten cows for them. *Cupa cupa!"*

Ndama's hopes were now so high he began to work up courage to talk about Bwana Green. He had just started to speak when Libuki jumped almost straight up in the air.

"Ach! Ach! Ach!" he exclaimed, grabbing his jaw. "My tooth! My tooth! Ach! Ach! Ach!" He paced back and forth, his eyes closed in agony. And then, shaking Ndama by the shoulder, he demanded, "What do you mean by making *obusuma* with rocks in it! Ach! Ach! Ach!"

"I-I'm s-sorry," stammered Ndama. "I-I-I didn't m-m-mean–"

"That doesn't help my toothache!" shouted Libuki. "Ach! Ach! Go call the witch doctor!"

Ndama ran down the path to Baku's hut and soon was back with the witch doctor. Baku knelt down by him and asked him to open his mouth. "It's the last tooth in the very back of your jaw," murmured the medicine man. "I'll have to pry it out with a knife. Hold still while I work."

He stuck a dull slender knife between the offending tooth and the next one and began to pry back and forth. But the tooth refused to budge. Then he picked up a heavy rock, placed the end of the knife on the tooth and began to pound.

"Ach! Ach! Don't do that," groaned Libuki. "I-I'd rather be dead than have you do that!"

Nevertheless the witch doctor continued.

Libuki endured the pounding for a fierce moment, and then he screamed. "Stop it! I told you to quit! Go on home, you don't know anything except to make pain!"

The witch doctor gathered up his knives and fled, not wanting to argue with such a strong man.

"Now what are you going to do?" asked Ndama, hoping his father would mention Bwana Green, the mission doctor.

"I-I don't know. B-but I can't stand this pain much longer."

"Why don't you go to Bwana Green?" Ndama dared to ask. "He'll pull the tooth and you won't have any pain at all. He has wonderful *dowa*."

"B-but I-I don't like– Ach! Ach!...

"Take me to him, I can't stand this pain anymore!"

Bwana Green put a needle in Libuki's mouth and squeezed some medicine into his gum. "After awhile your jaw will feel like a piece of wood," said the missionary gently. "When it does, tell me."

Libuki stared at Ndama and Ochella with real terror leaping from his eyes, for this was the first time a white man had ever touched him. Ndama held his hand in order to calm him.

In a few minutes Libuki said, "Bwana White Man, my face feels like that of a dead man."

"That's just what I wanted to hear," said Green. He slipped his forceps over the tooth and began to twist back and forth. In a moment the big molar was out.

"When are you going to pull it?" asked Libuki after Green had stepped back.

"There it is!" said Green, holding it out to him in his shiny forceps.

"But it can't be," muttered Libuki. "I didn't feel any pain."

"Hold out your hand," said Green.

Libuki picked up the decayed tooth and looked at it with amazement. Then the real truth of the matter sank into his brain. "It's out! It's out! My tooth is out!" he fairly shouted. "My tooth is out and I didn't feel any pain."

With a quick movement he grabbed Ochella and Ndama by their hands. "If Bwana Green has this much wisdom you must work for him and with him as much as you can," he said. "And whenever Bwana White Man goes on a trip I hope you can go with him. He's wonderful!"

"I'm not the one who is wonderful," replied Green modestly. "The wonderful one is Jesu Christo! He is the one who sent me to Africa and helped your sons to become such brave and good boys!"

10   At the Post Office

WHERE ARE YOU going?" asked Ndama after Green had shifted gears.

"I think we'd better go to Kisumu first," replied the missionary. "I'll have to get a new helmet and pick up the mail. I wrote to our mission board some weeks ago about sending a new missionary, and it's about time for a reply."

"Do you think they might be able to send someone to help the Luo?" asked Ochella.

"I-I don't know," returned Green thoughtfully. "I certainly hope so."

Green parked his truck by the little corrugated-iron post office and went in with the brothers to get his mail. Several ships had come into Mombasa a few days before and so there were many letters. He took the pile out to the car, and then picked out a long brown envelope. This one was from the missionary board. Quickly he scanned the crisp letter, and then his face fell.

"What's the trouble, Bwana Green?" asked Ndama.

The missionary stared at the letter for a long moment before answering and then with a hoarseness in his voice he said, "They have a young man and his wife who want to come but there is no money to send them!"

"Does this mean that no one will go to the Luo?" asked Ndama.

"I guess so."

"That's terrible," put in Ochella. "They're so ready for the gospel, and yet we can't take it to them."

"And the pitiful thing is that there are hundreds of other tribes who have to be neglected just like the Luo. Sometimes there's no money, and sometimes there's no one who wants to go. Oh, I wish God would move people's hearts to do something."

Suddenly Ndama pointed to another envelope that looked just like the first. "There's another letter from the mission board," he said.

Green snatched at it like a hawk snatching a baby chick. He ripped it open and withdrew another crisp sheet of paper. Then his face lit up.

"What is it?" shouted Ndama excitedly.

"The letter says that a church in Omaha, Nebraska has raised enough money to send us a man and his wife, and they have promised to support them after they get here! Isn't that wonderful? Let's thank God right now!"

The three of them prayed together right in the truck, and then they headed for Bunyore. As they speeded down the road that curved around the lake toward the mission, Bwana Green kept exclaiming, "Just think, the Luo will have a teacher! Just think, the Luo will have a teacher!"

Then Ochella tapped him on the shoulder. "Bwana Green," he said, "you forgot to buy that new hat!"

"I'll get it next time," laughed the missionary. "I'm too happy right now to be buying hats!"